Gary Cookson
The Squeezed Middle

Middle Management Matters

Series Editor
Roderick Millar

Volume 1

Gary Cookson

The Squeezed Middle

How to succeed in the critical role of a middle manager

DE GRUYTER

ISBN 978-3-11-171326-7
E-ISBN (PDF) 978-3-11-171352-6
E-ISBN (EPUB) 978-3-11-171374-8
ISSN 3052-2498
e-ISSN 3052-2501

Library of Congress Control Number: 2025950998

Bibliographic information published by the Deutsche Nationalbibliothek
The Deutsche Nationalbibliothek lists this publication in the Deutsche Nationalbibliografie;
detailed bibliographic data are available on the Internet at http://dnb.dnb.de.

© 2026 Walter de Gruyter GmbH, Berlin/Boston, Genthiner Straße 13, 10785 Berlin
Cover image: Dörte Nielandt, Berlin
Typesetting: Integra Software Services Pvt. Ltd.

www.degruyterbrill.com
Questions about General Product Safety Regulation:
productsafety@degruyterbrill.com

"I told you not to write another book, don't think I won't find out if you do it again", was the warning from my wife Katie after I wrote my second book. I tried to keep this one secret from her but she has ways of finding out, and was kind enough to pretend that she didn't know what I was doing. She gives me so much support and guidance in life, and in work, that I don't know what I'd do without her.

My children – Owen, Faye, Poppy, and William – all remain blissfully ignorant of what I do for a living, though they are happy each time they appear in a Dedication, and they remain inspirations to me.

My Dad, ever the pragmatist, wonders if writing another book takes me away from "proper work" and whether it helps with retirement planning, but reminds me that my Mum would certainly have approved 100%.

My family – I wouldn't be without them.

Foreword

By Ed Monk, CEO & Co-Founder, LPI – the Global Body for Workplace Learning

Middle management is one of the most misunderstood, underappreciated, and yet mission-critical layers of any organisation. These individuals operate at the intersection of strategy and execution, people and process, vision and reality. They are expected to deliver results, support teams, manage upwards, and adapt to relentless change, all while rarely receiving the support, recognition, or development they deserve.

That is why this book matters.

In this timely and important work, Gary shines a long-overdue spotlight on the realities of being a middle manager. Across eight insightful chapters, the reader is taken on a journey through the unique pressures, skills, opportunities, and future relevance of middle management. Each chapter is grounded in research, informed by experience, and filled with practical insights that will resonate with anyone who has worked in, managed, or relied upon this crucial level of leadership.

What makes this book stand out is not just the clarity of its structure or the wealth of case studies, but the empathy with which it is written. **Gary** really understands the emotional labour involved in middle management: the constant juggling of priorities, the strain of being both support and shield, the weight of decisions that often go unrecognised. That understanding gives this book an authenticity and relevance that is rare.

Gary is unquestionably, exceptionally well-placed to write this book. With extensive experience working alongside middle managers across multiple sectors, and a deep understanding of leadership development, his insights are both informed and credible. The inclusion of real voices from organisations such as Yorkshire Water, Knight Frank, and leading construction and retail firms adds depth and immediacy, elevating the book beyond theory into something human and applicable. No surprise here, as Gary is an evangelist for lifelong learning.

Throughout, the book explores themes that I personally believe are essential to the future of work.

First, there is the theme of complexity. Today's organisations are not only operating in volatile and ambiguous environments; they are increasingly fluid in structure and purpose. In this context, middle managers must learn to navigate ambiguity, build informal influence, and make decisions without always having perfect clarity. This book equips them to do just that.

Second, the theme of skills runs throughout. Not just technical or operational skills, but what **Gary** rightly calls "smarter skills": emotional intelligence, adapt-

https://doi.org/10.1515/9783111713526-202

ability, reflection, and the ability to lead others through change. These are not soft skills. They are core skills. They are the ones that artificial intelligence cannot replicate and that define truly effective leadership at every level.

Third is the theme of learnership, a concept that is close to my own heart. As I have written myself elsewhere, learnership is about leading through learning: modelling curiosity, growth, and humility in a fast-changing world. This book positions learnership as a central, enabling force for middle managers. It shows how those in the middle must not only manage the learning of others but engage in their own ongoing development if they are to stay relevant and resilient.

And finally, there is the theme of possibility. Despite the challenges facing middle managers, and they are many, this book offers hope. It provides tools, language, and encouragement for middle managers to reimagine their role not as stuck between the top and bottom, but as uniquely positioned to influence culture, performance, and transformation. In doing so, the book is as much a call to action for senior leaders as it is a guide for middle managers themselves.

The chapters are thoughtfully constructed. From the opening exploration of middle management complexity to the closing reflections on their future, each section builds on the last. The chapters on hybrid work and emotional intelligence are particularly pertinent to today's workplace, while the insights into coaching, mentoring, and psychological safety offer practical advice that any organisation would do well to heed.

What we should also appreciate is the book's pragmatic optimism. It does not shy away from the difficulties, nor does it romanticise the role. Instead, it offers a grounded path forward: one that involves continuous development, thoughtful leadership, and the creation of supportive cultures where middle managers can thrive. The examples of tailored development programmes, peer networks, and coaching support bring this to life in vivid detail.

As someone who has spent years working in the field of leadership and learning, I believe we are entering a new era. One where titles matter less and behaviours matter more. One where those closest to people and performance, our middle managers, need to be empowered, developed, and valued as key drivers of organisational success.

This book is a contribution to that shift. It invites us to see middle management not as a rung to move past, but as a vital leadership space in its own right. It invites organisations to reimagine how they support this population. And it invites middle managers themselves to grow, reflect, adapt, and lead with renewed purpose.

If you are a middle manager, this book will speak to your lived experience and offer tools to navigate it with greater confidence. If you support or lead middle managers, it will help you understand their reality and better equip them for success. And if you care about the future of work, a future in which human leadership is more important than ever, then this book is essential reading.

I am proud to introduce it.

Preface

What this book is about

In the world of work, the middle manager is often an unsung hero – a lynch-pin bridging strategic vision with practical execution, and a shield that absorbs the chaos from above while maintaining order below. But despite their pivotal role middle managers are frequently overlooked, undervalued, and left to navigate shifting workplace dynamics with little more than instinct and, if they are lucky, resilience.

Over the past few years, the role of middle management has undergone a seismic transformation. The rise of hybrid work, rapid technological advancements, and evolving employee expectations have reshaped the workplace landscape. No longer is it enough to simply "manage." Today's middle managers must lead with empathy, adapt to uncertainty, and drive change – all while delivering results. They are simultaneously strategists, coaches, culture builders, and caretakers.

I wrote this book to shine a spotlight on the reality of being a middle manager in the modern world of work, and to equip those in this challenging position with the tools, strategies, and mindsets they need to thrive. It is not a handbook filled with one-size-fits-all solutions. Instead, it is a guide grounded in the realities of modern work, offering practical insights and frameworks that middle managers can adapt to their unique contexts.

In writing this book, I have drawn on research, case studies, and my own experiences working with and supporting middle managers across industries. Each chapter addresses a critical aspect of the role, from bridging strategy and execution to managing change, fostering high-performing teams, and cultivating emotional intelligence. These are not abstract concepts; they are the skills and attributes that define the modern middle manager.

One of the key themes running through this book is adaptability. The world of work is changing faster than ever, and the ability to pivot, learn, and grow is no longer optional, but essential. This is true not only for middle managers themselves but also for the teams they lead. A culture of continuous learning and resilience is the bedrock of a successful team, and middle managers are uniquely positioned to create and sustain this culture.

Another central theme is the human side of management. Behind every strategy, project, and goal are people – individuals with hopes, challenges, and potential. Middle managers can unlock this potential, empower their teams, and leave a lasting impact on their organizations. This book celebrates that opportunity while acknowledging the pressures and complexities that come with it.

https://doi.org/10.1515/9783111713526-203

As you read through these chapters, I hope you will find not only practical advice but also a sense of camaraderie and encouragement. Middle management is often called the "squeezed middle," but I prefer to think of it as the "magnificent middle" (a phrase borrowed from one of the case studies within the book). It is a role that demands incredible skill, resilience, and vision. It is also a role that has the power to shape the future of work.

To the middle managers reading this: you are not alone. You are part of a vast, often unseen network of individuals facing similar challenges and striving for excellence. This book is my contribution to your journey – a roadmap to help you navigate the complexities of your role and achieve your full potential.

To leaders, HR and L&D professionals, and anyone who works closely with middle managers: this book is an invitation to understand, support, and invest in these vital contributors to organizational success.

Middle management is not a stepping stone; it is a destination. It is a career path filled with opportunity, challenge, and impact. My hope is that this book will empower you to embrace that path with confidence, clarity, and purpose.

Let's get started.

Who I am and why I wrote this.

As someone who has spent my career immersed in the dynamics of leadership, organizational design, and the future of work, I've had the privilege of working closely with middle managers across industries. From leading workshops on organizational transformation to consulting with teams navigating hybrid work, I've seen firsthand the pressures middle managers face and the incredible impact they can have when equipped with the right support. My work has always been driven by a belief that middle management is not just a transitional role – it is a vital, pivotal one.

I am also the author of *Making Hybrid Working Work, and HR for Hybrid Working*, manifestos for navigating the modern workplace exploring the intersection of culture, leadership, and flexibility. Through my writing, speaking engagements, and consulting practice, I've dedicated my efforts to understanding how organizations thrive – and at the heart of it, how people make it happen. This book builds on that foundation, focusing specifically on the challenges and opportunities facing middle managers today.

How the book works

This book offers a roadmap for navigating the complexities of middle management, blending actionable insights with practical tools to help you thrive in this pivotal role.

We begin by addressing the dilemmas of middle management, uncovering the pressures and opportunities of being at the organizational crossroads. From there, we explore bridging strategy and execution, equipping you to align high-level goals with team outcomes. Leadership takes centre stage in chapters on building leadership in the middle and managing change, offering guidance on fostering resilience, adaptability, and team success. We then focus on the people factor, emphasizing mentorship, team building, and collaboration, followed by a deep dive into emotional intelligence and soft skills – the human side of management. Finally, we tackle leading in a hybrid world and continuous growth, providing tools to navigate remote work, foster lifelong learning, and adapt to ever-changing demands.

Each chapter will have a similar structure:

- The detail of the chapter. This will also include research compiled for this book from experts, thought leaders and leading thinkers, sharing their views on themes explored in relevant chapters. Each chapter is interspersed with examples that illustrate key points in real world situations.
- Case studies – stories from the front line, sharing what organisations have done, what worked and what did not. The majority of these are from named organisations. Some others will be from clients of my business EPIC, or other organisations, who prefer to remain anonymous for assorted reasons. In sharing these anonymous case studies some of the organisational characteristics may have been made more generic to further protect their anonymity.
- Case Study reflections – the main learning points to consider from each case study.
- The Action Plan – in building your practices further, and planning for actions you need to take to move forward on the issues examined in the chapter.
- References – further and wider reading and much of the evidence behind each chapter, linking to leading thinkers and thinking on the subjects discussed to help you apply the learning from reading this.

I'd love to hear from you as you read the book and/or after you are finished. Track me down on social media – BlueSky, Threads, or LinkedIn – and let me know your thoughts and questions.

Happy reading.

Acknowledgements

Firstly, thank you for buying and reading this book. As with all my books, I have enjoyed writing it, but I have written it for you – so I hope you enjoy reading it and can use the thoughts within it.

My family – my wife and four children primarily, but also my parents – have been instrumental in my whole life personally and professionally, giving me inspiration, motivation, and gratitude throughout. They have believed in me, even if not entirely sure what it is I do, and I am grateful again for their eternal support.

My publishers De Gruyter have believed in me and what I have wanted to say via their outlets. They have consistently supported me. I want to recognise the efforts of Roddy Millar (who first approached me with the idea for this book), Matthew Smith, and Maximilian Gessl.

Ed Monk has made a significant contribution to this book. His Foreword delighted me as his stature within the spheres of leadership, management, and learning, is beyond compare. I am privileged to call him a friend too, but to have him read and comment on my work is something else entirely. Without his contribution this book would have been much less than it is.

Within this book there are numerous people whose contributions to examples and case studies have brought it alive. They have given their time and thoughts willingly and without hesitation. In the order they appear in this book: Jo Carlin, Ryan Cheyne, Craig Fines-Allin, Anwen Bottois, Rachel Wood, Rick Bradley, Hannah Patchett, Wayne Ledden, Adrian Emmott, Meg Gorman, Wendy Thomas, Nick Holmes, Nancy Parks, Diane Allton, Karen Dolan, Megan Yawor, Rob Ashcroft, Sue Hughes, and Amy Batchelor. In addition, there are others, who have requested anonymity, but for whose contributions I am also grateful.

Lots of other people who contributed random comments and quotes and to all those mentioned in the book (and all those not mentioned), thank you for making them. A few more people helped by giving their time to peer review some chapters for me as I went along – and this helped me polish what you have in front of you. In no order: Cheri Brenton, Sharon Green, Marc Weedon, Anna Edmondson, Gail Hatfield, Ian Pettigrew, Veronica Richards, Tania Montero, Trish Sangster, Vania Jussara, Tim Mitchell, Sam Jenniges, David Bullock, Michelle Parry-Slater, Natasha Johnson, Kelly Davis, Lubna Taj Malik, Karen Sanders, Hannah Clark, and Tamasin Sutton.

Thank you again to many of my clients who have allowed me to anonymously use their experiences, and to my wider network for not just cheering me on along the way but for putting up with my constant mentions of how I'm doing and how it has been going whilst putting all this together. As I have said before, it is more exciting than I expected, authoring a book, and it is hard to keep that to myself.

https://doi.org/10.1515/9783111713526-204

Contents

Foreword —— VII

Preface —— XI

Acknowledgements —— XV

Chapter One
The Middle Manager's Reality —— 1
    The Challenges of Middle Management —— 2
        The Balancing Act —— 2
    Striking the Right Balance —— 7
        Translating Strategic Directives Into Team-Specific Goals —— 7
        Being Transparent Whilst Protecting the Team From Pressure —— 7
        Giving a Sense of Priority When there are Goal-Related Conflicts —— 8
        Placing the Right Focus on People —— 8
    What Happens if we Undervalue Middle Managers? —— 9
    Redefining The Middle Management Role —— 10
        Reducing The Administrative Burden —— 10
        Focusing More on Capability Building —— 11
        Professionalising Middle Management —— 13
    Helpful Tools, Frameworks, and Systems —— 13
    Case Studies —— 14
    Case Study Reflections —— 16
    Action plan —— 17
    References —— 18

Chapter Two
Eessential Skills For Thriving in the Middle —— 20
    Translating Strategy Into Action —— 20
    How to Manage the Impact Middle Managers Have —— 22
        Boundary Management —— 22
        Network Connections —— 23
        Checking-in —— 24
        Leveraging Technology —— 24
        Bridging Communication Gaps —— 25
        Managing Up —— 25
        Managing Down —— 26

Developing and Supporting Middle Managers to Bridge
Communication Gaps —— **27**
Closing the Gaps —— **27**
Using Data Better —— **29**
Overcoming Misalignment —— **31**
Case Studies —— **31**
Case Study Reflections —— **33**
Action Plan —— **34**
References —— **34**

Chapter Three
Building Leadership In The Middle —— 36
Leading From The Middle —— **36**
Leading Laterally – Influencing Without Authority —— **39**
Balancing Managing Up With Managing Down —— **40**
Critical Leadership Skills to Develop in Middle Managers —— **42**
Emotional Intelligence (Ei) —— **43**
Change Management and Communication Skills —— **44**
Resilience —— **45**
High-Performance Cultures and Middle Managers —— **46**
Trust in Middle Managers —— **47**
Case Studies —— **49**
Case study refletions —— **50**
Action plan —— **51**
References —— **52**

Chapter Four
Leading In Transition – Embracing Change —— 53
The Role of Middle Management in Organisational Change —— **53**
Middle Managers and Handling Resistance to Change —— **57**
Empathy —— **58**
Communication —— **58**
Involvement —— **59**
Strategies to Align Teams Behind Change —— **60**
How Middle Managers Can Maintain Morale and Engagement During
Change —— **62**
Tools and Frameworks for Middle Managers to use During Change —— **63**

Case studies —— 65
Case study reflections —— 66
Action Plan —— 66
References —— 67

Chapter Five
Emotional Intelligence In Middle Management —— 68
The Importance of Ei —— 68
Developing Middle Manager Self-Awareness —— 73
Resolving conflict and EI —— 75
Communication and EI —— 77
Case Studies —— 79
Case Study Reflections —— 80
Action Plan —— 81
References —— 81

Chapter Six
The People Factor —— 83
Why are Coaching and Mentoring Essential Skills For Middle
Managers? —— 83
    Coaching —— 83
    Mentoring —— 84
Balancing Coaching and Mentoring with other Middle Management
Responsibilities —— 85
Developing Individuals and Teams Using Coaching, Mentoring, and other
Techniques —— 87
Helping Middle Managers To Be Better Coaches and Mentors to Develop
Their Teams —— 90
    Learnership —— 90
    Tools and Techniques —— 91
Case Studies —— 92
Case Study Reflections —— 94
Action Plan —— 94
References —— 95

Chapter Seven
Mastering Hybrid Work – Leading From Anywhere —— 96
   The Challenges that Remote and Hybrid Working Pose for Middle
   Managers —— **96**
   Fostering Collaboration and Enhancing Inclusion in a Hybrid Working
   Environment —— **100**
       Fostering Collaboration —— **101**
       Enhancing Inclusion —— **102**
   Using Technology and Data to Manage Hybrid Teams —— **103**
   Maintaining Productivity and Accountability in Hybrid Working —— **105**
   Critical Leadership Behaviours for Hybrid Working —— **108**
   Case Studies —— **110**
   Case Study Reflections —— **112**
   Action Plan —— **113**
   References —— **113**

Chapter Eight
The Future of Middle Management —— 115
   Adaptability – The New Core Middle Management Skill? —— **115**
   Fostering a Culture of Continuous Learning —— **118**
   Building Resilience and a Growth Mindset in Middle Managers —— **120**
   Staying Relevant as a Middle Manager —— **121**
       Artificial Intelligence and Middle Management —— **121**
       Softer Skills – or Smarter Skills? Emotional Intelligence and the Middle
       Manager —— **122**
   The Benefits of Continual Learning for Middle Managers and Their
   Teams —— **123**
   Case Studies —— **125**
   Case Study Reflections —— **127**
   Action Plan —— **127**
   References —— **128**

Index —— 129

Chapter One
The Middle Manager's Reality

Do you know anyone whose career aspiration was to be a middle manager? Was it your aspiration? I've been a middle manager, and other types of manager too. Not once during career discussions when in formal education did anyone mention middle management to me as a destination, or even a milestone on a journey to something else. In my research for this book, I've not come across anyone else who thought, whilst growing up, that they wanted to be a middle manager. And yet, research suggests that an average of 16% of the global workforce is considered one (Tucker, 2023). Of course, some of those are merely passing through on the way to being senior or executive leaders, but that is still a substantial number. Roughly one in six working people are middle managers. And you will struggle to find even one of them who wanted that.

Middle managers are numerous, and there will be organisations that are heavily loaded with such roles, compared to other organisations that may have fewer or none. Size matters. There is no official definition of middle management either, explaining why it does not often show in careers pathway discussions. It is often viewed as a stepping-stone, not a destination. We are not meant to stop there, but clearly many do. Middle management is often derided in public, and amongst the first roles to suffer when organisations need to make cuts. Often though, those organisations come to regret de-layering in such ways and invest again in middle management once the short-term financial peril has passed. This tells us something about the unique and valuable role a middle manager plays.

In this book I will define a middle manager as someone who fulfils certain criteria:
1. They are not an executive, or part of the top team in an organisation.
2. They are responsible for a team and have at least one other manager reporting to them.

And that is it. If you fulfil those criteria, you are a middle manager and this book is for you. Or you are someone who has responsibility for developing middle managers – this book is also for you. Let's examine the unique challenges that middle managers face.

https://doi.org/10.1515/9783111713526-001

The Challenges of Middle Management

As the title of this book suggests, middle managers are often "the squeezed middle," balancing strategic priorities from above with the operational needs from below. Depending on the organisation, they may have unclear authority and influences over processes and outcomes. They must manage performance and morale for multiple layers beneath them, without being the ultimate decision-maker. McKinsey research suggests that 44% of middle managers have a negative experience with organisational bureaucracy and are overwhelmed with administration work whilst feeling a lack of empowerment and hampered decision-making (Field, Hancock and Quintero, 2024). It is enough to put anyone off being a middle manager, but it should not. This is a unique blend of challenges that middle managers can navigate, and successfully too, if they are supported and have a growth mindset. But research suggests that 52% of the working population don't see management as a valid career path, and that 54% of those who don't want to become managers suggest that it is the perception of too much stress in the role that is putting them off (Jacobs, 2025).

The Balancing Act

Middle managers are necessary in organisations over a certain size. When an organisation reaches the size where it needs at least five layers (CEO or similar; Executives; Middle Managers; First Line Managers/Supervisors; Front Line Staff), middle managers provider the glue that bind the layers together. They become responsible for balancing the organisational strategic direction, with helping their direct reports to motivate and develop their people, build, and utilise connections across the organisation, and highlighting the culture and values of the organisation. But, as a result, they can be conflicted and at risk of burnout and find it difficult to demonstrate their value or find time to grow themselves as leaders. Harvard Business Review suggested that middle managers are in the bottom 5% when it comes to job satisfaction (Zenger and Folkman, 2014), and SHRM research found that middle managers are more depressed than those in the layers above or below them (Wilkie, 2023). I often find first line managers who have been promoted to that position on the basis that they are the best person doing the jobs that report to that position, and it is remarkably similar for middle managers. Many in middle management positions have been promoted to that position on the basis that they were great at being first line managers or supervisors, or on the basis that their professional or technical knowledge of what the team does is high. It is no wonder that some are depressed – little preparation is given to most middle managers on what the role entails. It is different to other layers, and most learn on the job.

___

Jo Carlin is the European HR Director with a career spanning three decades, much of which has come in organisations with a global reach. She spoke to me about her time as a middle manager and in developing middle managers across her career.

Carlin describes organisational focus on middle managers like that we might pay a distant relative – someone we are aware that exists, and exchange occasional pleasantries with or see on special occasions, but otherwise we pay them hardly any attention and they are not in our thoughts. She also feels that middle management itself is not an exciting part of anyone's career, compared to one's first managerial position, or perhaps becoming a senior leader, with Carlin describing time spent as a middle manager to being in a holding pattern – some will emerge like butterflies into senior leadership, but many won't. In Carlin's experience, few organisations do this well, and she has likened it to watching a poor reality TV show – fascinating and groan-inducing in equal measure.

In Carlin's experience, middle management rewards are often not worth the effort. Good middle managers get lots of cross-organisational experience on multiple projects, selected because they are competent, but then struggle to manage the amount of work they have. And the bad ones are left to flounder. Consequently, she has seen organisations decide that middle managers are not needed any more, having realised that many of them simply shuffle things around the organisation rather than advancing its cause. Carlin has seen some organisations bypass middle managers completely and describes the plight of such middle managers as like salmon swimming upstream, with many not being strong enough to do that.

Carlin expanded on the impact of good middle managers being moved into project work due to their competence. Despite the volume of work they face, she feels this is a good thing for a middle manager as it helps develop their resilience because they will face a fast-moving, constantly changing environment, and experience lots of different team dynamics. She feels that it is possible to develop good middle managers but that there is an element of luck in this. She recommends that organisations have individualised career plans for their employees so that middle management is seen as a destination, with clearly defined parameters that individuals can assess for themselves whether needs to be on their journey.

In one of Carlin's previous organisations, a large redundancy programme was underway. This required that organisation to identify and focus on competent middle managers, since they would be needed to manage much of that programme. It prompted lots of conversations about who would be good at the people side of managing teams affected by redundancy, and who would be good subject matter experts if the people side would not be good for them. This enabled the organisation to develop the right people into its remaining middle management positions and deliver the right outcomes from the redundancy programme. But Carlin describes this as a "backs against the wall" decision rather than a strategic and foresighted one – though it shows that organisations can identify and focus on the right middle management skills when they need to. Carlin reminds us that if we are not strategic and foresighted we would lose the best middle managers before we need them.

Interestingly, when I asked Carlin about her best and worst experiences in her career, both came from her time as a middle manager. This is like my best and worst experiences too. Both Carlin and I had experiences where we felt we were the same person, with the same skills and knowledge, doing the same things, but the context for these experiences was quite different. This suggests that there is both a nature and nurture element to being successful in middle management. In both our positive experiences, the context provided scope to the role, variety, challenge, autonomy, empowerment, and a great role model from our senior leader.

Carlin concluded by saying that she believes few middle managers really know what they are doing or supposed to be doing, but the best ones know who to ask or where to find the answers – they leverage their network, and they help others to grow in order to develop future answers to problems. Too much is left to chance by organisations, in Carlin's experience – we are not always clear what a middle manager should be.

In the example above we see how much with middle management is left to chance, or decisions made too late. There is a need to train middle managers, if not before they take on the role, then as soon as possible afterwards. Time is a big consideration here, as are scale and budget, and there will be differing situations across organisations on both. However, it is worth doing – McKinsey research found that organisations with stronger middle managers realise twenty-one times greater Total Shareholder Return (TSR) compared to those with weaker middle managers (Field et al, 2023). This is because the role carries enormous responsibility and has impact on relationships and engagement across the organisation, and on organisational health in general. Development is therefore much recommended, blending different methods including formal and informal routes. Development should also focus on consistency of approach across middle managers. Whilst they may have their own sections to run with specific responsibilities, working on collective duties and responsibilities, the skillsets required to deliver those, and building a programme to develop and standardise these, would be helpful. Such development could bring greater role clarity and develop shared goals and ways of working towards those.

Ryan Cheyne has been both a middle manager and an executive in various large UK-based retail organisations and currently is an experienced interim manager working across multiple industries. He spoke to me about his experiences across multiple organisations and his role in developing middle managers over several decades. Middle managers in Cheyne's retail organisation were both Store Managers (who had Assistant Managers and Supervisors reporting to them) or Area Managers (to whom the Store Managers reported).

In Cheyne's own experience earlier in his career, he was not trained on how to be a manager, and his preparation for management consisted of process, policy and procedural training – his view was that people around him were promoted into middle management roles simply by demonstrating competence at roles reporting to the middle manager role. This experience taught him what principles he wanted to follow when he became responsible for developing middle managers – that middle managers need preparation for the role, that the development needs to focus on managing people and teams, and that this should continue once in role.

As Cheyne took on more responsibility for developing middle managers in one large UK-based retailer, he observed that too much was being left to chance, much like his previous firsthand experiences. As a result, attrition at middle manager level was much higher than at other levels, which

Cheyne attributed to the lack of preparation and some poor recruitment practices. He also identified some cultural issues – middle managers were not encouraged to coach their direct reports – and some structural issues too – in that Area Managers had an average of 25 Store Managers reporting to them, making quality time with each person nigh impossible.

Cheyne's response to this situation was to create a Fast Track Store Manager career pathway, to begin training people for the rise to middle management before they became one. This was an assessed (Pass/Fail) route, with the assessment done by executives and focusing on the prospective middle manager's abilities in what are oft referred to as "softer skills." Those who passed were offered the next available middle management position, and those who failed were offered more development and the opportunity to try the route again in the future. The programme lasted 6 months before anyone was deemed ready to take up a middle management position and was successful at tackling the high attrition at that level since it exposed candidates to the realities of being a middle manager. For those who opted out of the program having realised that middle management was not for them, the organisation created "individual contributor" roles to retain the specialist knowledge of such people.

Realising that good middle management is as much about relationships – the who, not the what – Cheyne also changed the spans of control, reducing from twenty-five, to somewhere between 10–15 direct reports per Area Manager. He encouraged them to spend the newly available time to coach, mentor and develop their direct reports and their teams. He acknowledged that the changes to spans of control increased the number of middle managers but said that the data showed that this move paid off in terms of cultural improvement and overall efficiencies.

Cheyne feels that middle managers are an "easy" target for companies that need to make financial savings. The executive level is often seen as untouchable, and similarly so are front-line services, leaving middle managers as the obvious targets rather than focusing on savings elsewhere through process change or innovation. When that has happened in Cheyne's organisations, he has observed a chasm created between the executive and first line managers that used to be filled by middle managers. He noticed that both felt increased pressure due to the absence of middle managers, as did support services like HR, Finance etc.

In the above example, we see how in many organisations one of the best ways to understand the value created by middle managers, is to try managing without them. We also see how structured and planned development can aid much of the issues faced by middle managers as they progress into that role.

It could also reduce the sense of isolation many middle managers feel. As a middle manager, one can often feel like the only person dealing with the precise balance of responsibilities and feeling that type of pressure. You are not the only person, but middle managers do not often get together with their peers to discuss what middle management is and how they are approaching it. Instead, focus is (often rightly) given to operational needs, and strategic priorities. But a development programme and the creation of a community of practice for middle managers could overcome this. Yet in an SHRM survey, only 20% said that their organisations helped them to be more successful as managers (SHRM, 2018).

In the middle management role, there can be a perfect storm of potentially negative circumstances. They must communicate organisational goals, direction, and policies. But they also must motivate employees to follow such things, and work with them if they dislike them (regardless of what personal view the middle manager may have on such things). A good example of this balancing act can be seen in organisations where, in recent years, there have been "return to office" (RTO) mandates. Often, such mandates come from the very top of the organisation and represent the opinions of the executives. Middle managers must implement such mandates. Microsoft examined this and found that 35% of managers had no personal preference about how often employees came onsite but felt that they had to follow company policy regardless (Bagnara, 2021). And yet despite this, middle managers are often amongst the first target for cuts when things do not go well for the organisation! And such cuts are regular, cyclical even. A study in the Academy of Management Executive talked about why middle management roles are undervalued and often the first to be targeted for cuts – in 1994! (Floyd and Wooldridge, 1994). Other articles decrying the cuts to middle management roles have been written in 1977!

The balancing act becomes harder with potentially unnecessary administrative tasks, which can take up a sizeable portion of middle management time. McKinsey estimates that middle managers spend 49% of their time on non-managerial work (McKinsey, cited in SHRM, 2018), which along with time spent in meetings, distracts them from doing what middle managers should and could be doing. To help, we need to streamline processes and reduce the administrative burden, whilst upskilling organisations to work asynchronously instead of holding out for meetings. This would enable middle managers to spend more time focusing on strengthening relationships (the who, rather than the what, perhaps) and providing that vital link between strategy and operations. Further research by McKinsey shows that workplace relationships account for 39% of employee job satisfaction, yet managers only devote 25% of their time to it (Allas and Schaninger, 2020). But when middle managers can spend more time on relationships – on managing talent and team dynamics, and on inter-relationships between teams – they are achieving the balance that the organisation often sorely needs. And such things can happen at the same time as working on change management efforts and acting as employee advocates – both valuable middle management roles.

Striking the Right Balance

There are several ways in which middle managers can balance the conflict demands from executives and their teams. They can translate strategic directives into team-specific goals; they can be transparent whilst protecting the team from pressure; they can give a sense of priority when there are goal-related conflicts; and they can place the right focus on people. Let's examine these four things in more detail.

Translating Strategic Directives Into Team-Specific Goals

Often this is where the balancing act is most delicate. It is an area of risk too – unless an organisation's middle managers are consistent in how they do this, failure is possible. But this relies on middle managers being confident and effective communicators, and that is not always the case – in an HR Magazine survey only 31% felt "very confident" in their ability to communicate organisational strategy to staff (Woodman, 2024). It goes further than just informing the teams of what the organisational strategy is, it is about effectively gathering feedback from the teams to share with executives. But if only 31% feel confident doing this two-way communication, then there is a need for organisations to invest in developing middle managers to have the professional skills to communicate effectively. There is also a need to have a way to ensure clarity on what the organisational strategy is and how each role connects to and aligns with that.

Being Transparent Whilst Protecting the Team From Pressure

Pressure on teams may come with the territory. That does not make it right, but it might make it unavoidable, particularly in a turbulent organisation or industry. A great middle manager will be honest about the pressure their teams are facing and will not hide the details or direction from that team but will work with the team to ensure that their capacity to handle the pressure is increased. One thing that I have done in similar situations is to work out when the teams need to collaborate and work together, and when individuals need to do deep, focused work – and to ensure that no meetings take place on the latter days. In one organisation this led to "no meeting Fridays" and in another, to not sending emails on Friday afternoons or Monday mornings. Informal conversations and communications still took place, but nothing formal. My teams benefitted from the additional space and time this created and were more energised for the collaborative work in-between.

Middle managers can also inform and involve the team in decision-making. I have been coaching a middle manager on increasing the amount of consultation they do with their team on decisions that affect them. Whilst some of the team are resistant to that, feeling that the middle manager should just get on with it, the majority are receptive to the consultation (which happens via different methods) and appreciative of the effort.

Transparency also involves holding firm to one's own, and the organisational, values – especially in the face of concerns about pressure. Being clear on, and being explicit about, how values are helping decisions to be made, is a noticeable and effective tactic for a middle manager. Middle managers may need guidance on how to role model values-based decision-making, and how to be transparent about issues that may place the values of the team under threat. This may involve calling out behaviour from individuals, whether more senior or more junior, which are adding to pressure.

Another helpful action would be to be seen to be willing to challenge executives on behalf of the team if the pressure is becoming too much.

Giving a Sense of Priority When there are Goal-Related Conflicts

Middle managers need to provide clarity where there is uncertainty. There are numerous situations where goal-related conflicts may arise, and the middle manager may need to either mediate or arbitrate in such conflicts. The middle manager needs to work with the team at the appropriate time to establish a clear sense of priority to the work of multiple teams. As part of this, the middle manager should determine with the team what happens if two or more goals come into conflict – which would take priority, and why? Which goals can be paused or ceased entirely? Which goals must not be threatened at all costs, and what would need to be adjusted if that goal is under threat?

Placing the Right Focus on People

Managers have a massive impact on the engagement and wellbeing of their teams. Whilst the Covid-19 pandemic clearly accelerated and made this requirement more important, it has been a key focus for middle managers for a long time. I recall a time when I went through a divorce – a very messy, public situation. My manager at the time asked me what I needed. I didn't know. He told me that it was OK to take time to think about what I needed and outlined for me several directions I could go in in relation to work. I could take time off to deal with my personal situation. I could stay in work and work even harder to try to put my personal situation out of my mind. I could stay in work and be sad and grumpy for a while. He told me he would understand any of those things, and so would my colleagues and teams. He offered to help me with whatever came next, and in doing so demonstrated considerable empathy and understanding. Even now, 20 years later, I would run through brick walls for him. Work was more than just results, it was about kindness, honesty, empathy for that manager, and for me too after that. I became more aware of how I could do the same with my teams and increased the amount of time I would spend managing the person, the human being, instead of their performance. And that helps when there is conflict and stress.

When there are times of pressure, remembering that we are dealing with human beings is important.

What Happens if we Undervalue Middle Managers?

Middle managers have, repeatedly over the decades, been given a bad reputation. It is not a "sexy" profession or occupation. There can be a lack of visibility into the impact of middle managers on organisational success. However, we ignore and undervalue it at our peril. Research has shown that managers (in general) are the single biggest determinant of employee satisfaction, performance, and wellbeing (Field et al, 2023). If we remove middle managers, someone must do aspects of their work – or everyone might suffer.

Plenty of organisations choose to delayer, focusing on middle managers. In 2023, Mark Zuckerberg, CEO of Meta, created a "Year of Efficiency", stating that "I don't think you want a management structure that's just managers managing managers, managing managers, managing managers, managing the people who are doing the work." (Dell'Anna and Can Yilmax, 2025). Zuckerberg is not alone in holding those views, with Google and Amazon all removing layers of middle management in recent years. Whilst the focus of these organisations is on reducing their cost base, and clearly reducing numbers of management salaries is a quick way to do that, they should be mindful of the consequences (and explore other options too). Organisations could consider whether improving the quality of middle managers or working to improve the quality of what middle managers do, could deliver the same outcomes.

Middle managers are clearly under pressure – they must ensure that operational goals are realised, whilst people remain happy, and the organisation delivers profits (or whatever else matters to it). But research has shown that 71% of middle managers reported feeling overwhelmed, stressed and burnt out (Garcia, 2024).

The middle manager can be considered the glue that holds the organisation together. What happens if that glue is missing? The best way to assess the impact that a middle manager has is to see what happens without them there. Many teams could lose something that sparks their creativity, effectiveness, and efficiency. Internal communication could suffer, as could organisational stocks of leadership and organisational skills.

As far back as 1994, research into cost reductions because of middle management delayering cast doubt on whether the hoped-for reductions had been realised (Floyd and Wooldridge, 1984), suggesting that when delayering, organisations suffer from the loss in ways that often outweigh the immediate cost savings. This loss comes from the reduced capacity of the organisation, and its remaining managers, to translate corporate strategy into action, to co-ordinate the activities of different teams, and to report back when corrective action is needed. Executives can do these things but may find them a distraction from other executive activities. Further research from Floyd and Wooldridge suggested that organisations who retained middle management input into strategy saw higher financial performance, and greater ease of implementation of strategic goals (Floyd and Wooldridge, 1984). The situation has not really altered over 40 years later.

If middle managers are trusted, then this in turn engenders trust. Remove the middle manager, and we risk removing trust between the executives and the rest of the organisation. However, in the same research, only 31% of middle managers feel "important" to and trusted by executives in the organisation (Rock et al, 2016). Is this really the situation we want to perpetuate? Of course not, but how can we be different – be better?

Redefining The Middle Management Role

The role of the middle manager is ripe for redefinition. Here are some areas to focus on:

Reducing The Administrative Burden

One of the main bugbears for middle managers is the amount of unnecessary bureaucracy they must deal with. As McKinsey points out, middle managers often have a reputation for being bureaucratic, but "they aren't so much the cause of bureaucracy as a barometer for it" (Field et al, 2023). That is a useful way of look-ing at it – middle management is often where much bureaucracy ends up, but that's a symptom of something rather than middle managers being an identifiable cause. Organisations can tackle that and should. I mentioned earlier in this chap-ter about middle managers doing things to help their teams such as no-meeting and no-email days, and if spread across the organisation and all its layers this would have a positive impact on middle managers too. Greater utilisation of available and emerging technologies would also help – in my own life I make sig-nificant use of generative AI, and most in-house systems now have such function-ality built in. Whilst not everything could or should be automated, examining the "critical 20%" of tasks that take up 80% of middle managers time would be a good starting point.

The last point utilises the Pareto Principle to identify the more critical tasks that a middle manager undertakes. This type of analysis is often useful in identi-fying areas where there may be bottlenecks and pain points, and in reaching agreement on which tasks can be dealt with differently. Some tasks may be ripe for automation. Others could be delegated, outsourced, or stopped altogether. This may lead to conversations about the most appropriate span of control for a middle manager to have, as we saw in our example from Ryan Cheyne.

I would also recommend have some guidelines on what meetings are for as a way of reducing the administrative burden on middle managers. In Chapter 7 we will examine the benefits of asynchronous working, but having clear expectations about what synchronous meetings are for would help. For example, organisations could specify that middle managers should only have meetings that matter, with people who need to be there, with a clear agenda and purpose, and sufficient time before and afterwards to prepare and take necessary actions.

Changing the amount of bureaucratic work that middle managers do may en-able greater clarity on what the ideal focus of a middle manager should be. Con-sider answering the question "if we did reduce the amount of administrative work, what would that free middle managers up to do?." The answer is more focus on leading and motivating their teams, and some may need more support and development in this area.

Focusing More on Capability Building

Middle managers should excel at building individual capabilities, which in turn builds organisational capabilities and capacity too. If we follow through on reduc-ing administrative time, then middle managers will have more time to invest in their team members, coaching them and fostering growth. A useful analogy comes from Bryan Hancock, who made the comparison about the sporting world, where the head coach of sports teams is in effect a middle manager, and amongst the most visible and highly paid of all managers in that organisation, a testament to their abilities in building individual and team capabilities (Field et al, 2023). In sports teams, head coaches are exceptionally valued by their organisations because of the time and success they have in building teams and individual capabilities. If we create time and space for our middle managers to do the same, it could increase the value they create and the way they are seen in organisations.

Craig Fines-Allin now runs his own HR consultancy but spoke to me about his time as EMEA HR Director at a professional services and auditing organisation with 500 employees based mostly in the UK but also across Europe. The client-facing staff were, and still are, an entirely remote/field-based operation.

Fines-Allin noted that middle managers within the organisation had often been promoted into that position without any formal training and were becoming accidental blockers to progress. An example came during communications in times of change. Middle managers would consciously filter information coming from above them to prevent overload in their teams, but this meant teams didn't get all the information they needed, and didn't understand what was happening.

Fines-Allin built a 4-day training programme for those progressing into middle management. The content was deliberately tailored to each individual, who chose their own path through it, building their own timetable and content. The cohorts going through the programme were mentored by senior leaders and given genuine business projects to lead which helped them apply and embed their learning. The projects helped to make the training real and practical, and encouraged peer to peer learning and support, as well as increasing the effectiveness of relationships with senior leaders.

He also created a Managing Directors Advisory Council, a mixture of peer- or self-nominated employees who would meet quarterly with senior leaders. This helped to enable much more open communication, and more importantly helped reshape middle management behaviour. Feedback came from above and below that middle managers needed to change. Suddenly, middle managers realised that they shouldn't filter messages but pass them on, and help their teams to interpret the information, not shield them from it.

In the example above we see how a conscious focus on middle management capabilities can help to develop an identify and for them to thrive.

A strong focus should be placed on identifying opportunities for middle managers to lead change initiatives or improve processes, which improves visibility, clarity of decision-making and promotes capacity and capability building. Organisations with middle managers as owners of product lines, business processes and other parts of the organisational system that cut across functions will therefore be seen not as functional leaders, but leaders. Such moves will reinforce the importance of middle management to strategic objectives and value.

Professionalising Middle Management

Already in this chapter we have discussed developing middle managers. I would go further than this. Developing them is a great start, whether it is prior to becoming a middle manager or once they have become one. But with middle management not being seen by many as a destination, we need to clarify what it is. This may differ between organisations, but each organisation should decide what a middle manager does and is. They should determine what common, shared responsibilities middle managers have, and create dedicated communities of practice to sit alongside more formal structures for middle managers. The responsibilities should focus not on functional specific duties, but duties inherent in being a middle manager. That would enable those who, at earlier points in their career, want to excel in managing people, to have a clear aspirational point to aim for. The shared responsibilities would facilitate the building of strong cross-functional relationships to enhance the influence middle managers have.

This would help to rebrand the role from being a stepping stone, to a destination, and may also help to reduce the negative connotations associated with middle management. In a piece of research done by Katie Jacobs for People Management, various good practice examples were shared – role profiles for middle managers at an HR software company and including middle management duties in job descriptions at a financial institution (People Management, 2024). Adapting things like this will make it easier to spot potential middle managers – with great interpersonal skills, and elevated levels of problem-solving, conflict-resolution and decision-making ability – early on, finding people who are not simply good at it, but like doing it too.

Development could include both coaching and mentoring, as well as action learning support from the community of practice. It should include formal development options, and access to a range of self-study resources too, which could also be shared with the middle managers' teams. But what tools, frameworks and systems could help middle managers to grasp this redefined role?

Helpful Tools, Frameworks, and Systems

A middle manager should be well-supported to perform their task, and it is tempting to consider the potential for generative AI to do much of this support. Of course, it can. But that can't replace the human elements that are needed, and the way a middle manager thinks. Throughout the remainder of this book, we will look in more depth at many of the skillsets and mindsets required by modern middle managers. Here I will summarise some of the key aspects that you will read about sprinkled through later chapters:

- The McKinsey 7S tool offers middle managers a way to view the organisational alignment required for much of the initiatives they will be involved in.
- Time management software such as Microsoft Viva can help middle managers to identify time for focused work, how to minimise distractions, and create the right routines to manage work better.
- Knowledge management systems, including user-generated content and organisational Wikis, can provide ready access to resources to solve problems and address pain points in real time, whilst facilitating the asynchronous work middle managers need to be more comfortable with in the modern world of work.
- 360 feedback tools can help to examine the impact of middle management behaviour and identify any corrective action required.
- Motivational theories (both classic theories such as Herzberg and Maslow, and modern theories such as Pink's Drive and Marquet's Greatness), and coaching models such as GROW, will ensure middle managers are equipped to build capability and capacity in their teams.
- Difficult conversation frameworks, such as Fierce, and Situation-Behaviour-Impact (SBI), will equip middle managers to deal with anticipated and unanticipated tricky situations.
- Change management models, including Lewin, Kotter, ADKAR and more, would help middle managers guide their teams through change, minimise resistance and embrace new possibilities.
- Financial appraisal techniques, including Cost-Benefit Analysis, and ROI/ROE, will help middle managers navigate some of the complexities of decision-making and link their programs better to strategic goals.

In our next chapter, we will look at how middle managers bridge the gap between strategy and operations.

Case Studies

In this case study I will reflect on my own experiences in an organisation as a middle manager. The organisation, which no longer exists, was in the voluntary sector in the north-west of the UK and had approximately 500 employees during my time there. I was a middle manager there for over a decade, and in that layer of the organisation there were around 10 such roles.

The organisation had a well-defined executive team who had clear responsibilities in terms of setting strategic direction but also running the organisation.

That team had been through multiple iterations of a development programme, and there was always a range of support available for executives. Beneath my layer, there were around 40–50 first line managers and supervisors. These were called "operational managers" and again had clearly defined responsibilities around running their teams of assorted sizes and delivering services to our customers. This operational management group also had a noticeably clear development programme to support them in their roles. But for us middle managers, it felt as if we were neglected, forgotten. We had no development programme and there was no preparation for our role as middle managers. We had no clear responsibilities either – the tier above us, and the tier below us, both did – and whatever wasn't in either of their sets of responsibilities, fell to us.

Within the organisational structure this middle management tier had varying duties linked to operational delivery, and some vague statements about supporting the work of the executive team. We all felt it was unclear. We had no collective purpose, and no collective relationship or responsibilities in our role as middle managers, and we were drifting as a result.

The organisation, with my input, responded in several helpful ways:
– I developed a dedicated middle manager development programme. It included a range of methods such as workshops, coaching, action learning sets, and self-study resources. It was a mandatory programme on the basis that the organisation wished to ensure both consistency and that all middle managers were trained to the same level. It was externally accredited by the UK's Institute of Leadership and Management, leading to a Level 7 Award in Strategic Leadership. The programme focused on the skills and competencies that the organisation required from its middle managers, a selection of which is below, and placed emphasis on how to do these things collectively and develop consistency of approach:
    – Focus on organisational efficiencies and robust budget management
    – Benchmarking service delivery levels
    – Utilisation of modern technology to develop new ways of working
    – Mapping future workforce and skill requirements
    – Effective knowledge management processes
    – Leveraging procurement processes
    – Reviewing operational structures
    – Managing risk and safety issues in service delivery
    – Reviewing and improving processes
    – Coaching direct reports on becoming better managers
    – Effectively managing projects
    – Reviewing communication effectiveness across the service

- Creation of a standalone meeting structure for middle managers, ensuring that we all met together fortnightly. As part of this, clarity was given to our specific responsibilities both individually and, especially, collectively. This ensured that we were all working together on shared goals and had similar objectives for our individual goals. The collective responsibilities focused on running the organisation – allowing the executive team to refocus on organisational strategy and leaving us middle managers to deliver what the business needed.
- Linking performance related pay to the achievement of our collective responsibilities to encourage teamworking.
- Running an initiative to refresh organisational culture and values. Whilst this was a cross-section of the organisation and involved a lot more people, the middle management tier was given responsibility for sponsoring the programme and were expected to demonstrate visible involvement in it. Once it had concluded, we all had responsibility to identify individuals and teams adopting the revised values, and to reward and recognise them as such. It was our responsibility to ensure that the revised values were seen and felt through the entire organisation.
- Creating socialisation opportunities – we were encouraged to go out as a group on social events, and to utilise a range of informal communication channels such as dedicated WhatsApp groups that were just for middle managers. This helped to build the informal bonds we needed, and to reduce the sense of isolation we often felt.

These individual actions all helped but taken as a whole they transformed what it was to be a middle manager in the organisation. Suddenly, we had purpose, we had clarity, and we had empowerment. We were not just individual middle managers, but we had colleagues, a peer group, and shared goals and accountabilities. Engagement levels were consistently higher amongst middle managers than other groups in the organisation, and we went 8 years without any middle manager choosing to leave the organisation. The organisation itself became phenomenally successful, to the extent that it was eventually acquired by a larger organisation which thrives to this day.

Case Study Reflections

In the case study for this chapter, focusing on my own experiences as a middle manager in an organisation some years ago, the following points stand out for reflection:

- Role clarity is often neglected for middle managers, at the expense of tiers both above and below, but when delivered, can be empowering.
- Development for the role of a middle manager is necessary. It isn't an executive position, and it isn't an operational position. It blends elements of both, and support is necessary to create comfort and familiarity with that.
- Middle management is often an isolating position to be in. The creation of a community of practice, including both formal and informal communications and networks, can help to reduce this.
- Creating collective responsibilities focused on typical middle management responsibilities is extremely helpful. Linking to reward can be even more helpful if the circumstances allow.
- Middle managers have a key role to play in embedding organisational culture and values. They can often see more and can work together to ensure consistency of approach.

Action plan

If you are wanting to help middle managers to navigate the complexity of their position, or want to do so yourself, then the following questions will be helpful to answer:
- What is the experience, and reaction to that, of your middle managers?
- How much emphasis is placed on functional/technical expertise vs leadership abilities when recruiting middle managers?
- How could the organisation create time, space, and resources for a middle management development programme?
- What could be done for those with specialist and valued knowledge who don't want to become a middle manager?
- How effective are the current spans of control in your middle management groups?
- What groups, networks or forums allow (or could allow) for middle managers to come together to talk about the challenges of middle management?
- How can the administrative burden on middle management best be eased at your organisation?
- How will you focus middle management on relationship building, coaching, and mentoring?
- What level of communication skills do your middle managers need? What level do they have?
- How are middle managers expected to uphold organisational values?

- How clear are middle managers on the relative priority of differing strategic goals, and what should "give" when there is conflict?
- What would be the consequences of eliminating some/all middle managers from the organisational structure?
- How can you professionalise the middle management role?

References

Allas, T. and Schaninger, B. (2020) *The boss factor: Making the world a better place through workplace relationships, McKinsey & Company.* Available at: https://www.mckinsey.com/capabilities/people-and-organizational-performance/our-insights/the-boss-factor-making-the-world-a-better-place-through-workplace-relationships

Bagnara, G. (2021) *To thrive in hybrid work, support flexibility in work styles, To Thrive in Hybrid Work, Support Flexibility in Work Styles.* Available at: https://www.microsoft.com/en-us/worklab/work-trend-index/support-flexibility-in-work-styles

Tucker, E. (2023) *How many middle management positions do you need?, APQC.* Available at: https://www.apqc.org/blog/how-many-middle-management-positions-do-you-need

Dell'Anna, A. and Can Yilmaz, M. (2025) *High-stress, low reward: Why Gen Z is Shunning Middle Management Jobs, euronews.* Available at: https://www.euronews.com/my-europe/2025/01/21/high-stress-low-reward-why-gen-zs-are-shunning-middle-management-jobs

Field, E. *et al.* (2023) *Activating Middle Managers through capability building, McKinsey & Company.* Available at: https://www.mckinsey.com/capabilities/people-and-organizational-performance/our-insights/activating-middle-managers-through-capability-building

Hancock, B. and Field, E. (2023) *The Future of Middle Management, McKinsey & Company.* Available at: https://www.mckinsey.com/capabilities/people-and-organizational-performance/our-insights/the-future-of-middle-management

Field, E., Hancock, B. and Quintero, E. (2024) *Middle managers can succeed by simplifying the role, McKinsey & Company.* Available at: https://www.mckinsey.com/capabilities/people-and-organizational-performance/our-insights/the-organization-blog/middle-managers-can-succeed-by-simplifying-the-role

Field, E., Hancock, B., Smallets, S., *et al.* (2023) *Investing in middle managers pays off-literally, McKinsey & Company.* Available at: https://www.mckinsey.com/capabilities/people-and-organizational-performance/our-insights/investing-in-middle-managers-pays-off-literally

Floyd, S.W. and Wooldridge, B. (1994) 'Dinosaurs or Dynamos? recognizing middle management's strategic role', *Academy of Management Perspectives*, 8(4), pp. 47–57. doi:10.5465/ame.1994.9412071702.

Garcia, E. (2024) *Supporting middle managers: HR strategies to prevent burnout, Capterra.* Available at: https://www.capterra.co.uk/blog/4596/middle-manager-burnout-how-employers-can-support-them

Jacobs, K. (2024) *Under pressure: Why the 'squeezed middle' is having such a hard time – and what HR can do about it, Home.* Available at: https://www.peoplemanagement.co.uk/article/1894065/pressure-why-squeezed-middle-having-hard-time-%E2%80%93-hr

Jacobs, K. (2025) *The broken ladder, Investors in People.* Available at: https://www.investorsinpeople.com/knowledge/the-broken-ladder/

Rock, S. *et al*, (2020) *The Middle Manager Lifeline, CMI*. Available at: https://www.managers.org.uk/knowledge-and-insights/research/the-middle-manager-lifeline/

Wilkie, D. (2023) *The Miserable Middle Managers, Welcome to SHRM*. Available at: https://www.shrm.org/topics-tools/news/employee-relations/miserable-middle-managers

Woodman, P. (2024) *Boosting trust in your middle managers, HR Magazine*. Available at: https://www.hrmagazine.co.uk/content/features/boosting-trust-in-your-middle-managers/

Zenger, J. and Folkman, J. (2024) *Why middle managers are so unhappy, Harvard Business Review*. Available at: https://hbr.org/2014/11/why-middle-managers-are-so-unhappy

Chapter Two
Eessential Skills For Thriving in the Middle

Being in the middle could be a difficult place. It certainly does not sound easy. At the top, there is no-one to report to, to hold you accountable. At the bottom, there are no direct reports and no burden of responsibility for others. Even supervisory-level managers may find things more straightforward, with a smaller number of direct report and the relative ease of only having to think about what one team does. But middle managers, squeezed and/or stuck, that is not so easy. In this chapter we will examine what the skills are that middle managers need to acquire and deploy to thrive in that position. We will start with how they break down organisational goals into actionable tasks, how they communicate the "why" behind strategy to drive engagement, and how they monitor progress and ensure alignment across their various teams.

Translating Strategy Into Action

Despite temptations to reduce the middle management cadre, and moves to do so from some organisations, we must be mindful of the consequences of doing so. It may well reduce overheads, but middle managers are vital in guiding their organisations through change – and change is a constant in the modern world of work. Middle managers, when effective, bind their teams together by aligning their work with organisational direction, and provide the connection that both employees and the organisation need. But how does this happen? Certainly not by chance.

Where middle managers are included and involved in shaping organisational strategy, research has shown that this can enhance strategic decisions, generate greater consensus about strategy, and aid the smoother implementation of said strategy (Wooldridge and Floyd, 1990). The opposite must therefore be true also – if middle managers are not included or involved, it would harm or delay implementation, potentially undermining it completely. How effectively this inclusion and involvement is done depends on the interface between the senior teams and middle managers. It may take time, but effective relationships between those layers can make an enormous difference. Middle managers therefore not only have to develop and use great leadership and management skills to help those teams which report to them, but they must develop and use great upward-influencing skills to connect with and help the senior teams in their organisations. They are connectors. They are also, usually, subject matter experts, opera-

https://doi.org/10.1515/9783111713526-002

tional leaders, and people managers. No wonder middle managers often express their unhappiness and frustration with their position.

Anwen Bottois is currently a Leadership Development consultant but spoke to me about her time as a middle manager in two different organisations. The first was an energy/utilities company operating across the UK, and the other a higher education institution within the North of the UK. Her experience of becoming a middle manager was, like many others in this book, an almost accidental one and one that involved hardly any preparation, support, or training. However, Bottois feels that her natural personality traits of connecting well with others, coaching skills, and HR background, all helped her to swim rather than sink in middle management.

Whilst Bottois received an induction into both her middle management roles, this covered the technical aspects of the role and not the specifics of leading multiple teams, managing managers or any of the other key middle management responsibilities. Across both organisations there was an assumption that new middle managers could just do those things, and yet there was no clarity on what middle managers should be doing.

Too much was left to chance in Bottois' experiences, and she felt as if she had to figure things out as she went along – including how to manage up, down, and across, the organisation simultaneously – without being given sufficient capacity to think about how to do these things or to learn. She believes that not many organisations know what good is in terms of middle management, and many middle managers themselves are unconsciously incompetent at the role.

I asked Bottois what she now believes the middle management role to be. She feels that they should create environments where people can perform at their best; be a custodian of their people, something she sees as a privilege and not a chore; to have to want to help people develop and grow; and to build relationships and networks across the organisation.

Sadly, Bottois did not have these things provided for her. She felt isolated and underprepared as a middle manager in both organisations, despite sometimes having a great manager herself. She built her own network of other middle managers as well as accessing action learning sets and other forms of peer support, all of which she found useful. Her overriding memory of being a middle manager was that the recruitment, onboarding, and ongoing support of middle managers is sorely lacking in many organisations.

In the example above, we see some of the commonly shared frustrations in middle management experiences, and how many are left to sort this out for themselves.

As connectors, middle managers can often have several distinct aspects to understand and do well. This is succinctly captured in roles identified by Jaser, writing in Harvard Business Review (HBR, 2021), and summarised and adapted here. Middle managers must:

– Be able to look both ways in their organisation, empathising with senior leaders and with front line staff, and demonstrating understanding of the issues both face.
– Be able to explain the issues that senior leaders are wrestling with to front line staff, and vice versa, ensuring that all voices are heard and considered.

   –   Balance the needs of those above and below them, maintaining a clear sense of priority and clearly explaining that to all.

Much of the above aspects are best considered as conversation based. The frequency but more so the quality of the conversations middle managers have with their direct reports can improve performance and engagement. And the conversations middle managers have with senior leaders can help translate high level strategic priorities into operational realities, as well as connecting more easily to the organisational values. Middle managers need to be adept at having the right conversations, with the right people, at the right time.

What some middle managers may fail to grasp is that, as they become a middle manager, they may well have fewer direct reports, but their circle of influence expands dramatically both upwards and outwards (Training Industry, 2023). This influence affects all the individuals and teams that report to them but also the senior leaders to whom the middle manager now reports. Because of the range of functions a middle manager can have responsibility for, they are much more connected to wider organisational stakeholders and can take a broader view of how the organisation is functioning because they are likely to "see" more from their new position. But these new parts to their role are things for which they are likely under-prepared. Often middle managers are promoted to that position on the basis that they were good at the managing one team and delivering on operational targets. They would not have needed to do the things that a middle manager now needs to. Preparation, as covered in Chapter One, will be necessary. The middle manager plays a critical role in shaping and embedding organisational culture. They cast a shadow over a much larger area than any previous role, and it is easy to mismanage the impact that that has.

How to Manage the Impact Middle Managers Have

There are several things that will help. Boundary management, strong network connections, regular check-ins with stakeholders, making effective use of technology to automate the collection of performance data, and more. In this section we will discuss how to make these things work better.

Boundary Management

We talked in the previous section about the interfaces between senior teams and middle managers. Critical to the effectiveness of these interfaces is the trust that is built and flows between both parties. If middle managers trust that the senior leaders will seek and listen to their input on strategic matters and give the middle manager some autonomy in meeting targets, then engagement will usually result from that. The converse is also true – where trust is not in place, the middle manager may feel disengaged and disenfranchised. The autonomy a middle manager needs, which helps to build trust, can come from effective establishment of boundaries. These will help that middle manager to feel more psychologically safe in their role.

A middle management role can often seem nebulous, with unclear responsibilities. Spending time working these out explicitly – what does a middle manager control, and what do not they control – can be helpful to all concerned. Clarifying boundaries can help to organise communication and collaboration across distinct functions, whilst providing each middle manager with clear autonomy within their area of control. We must, though, be wary of developing silo-thinking. Encouraging middle managers to spend time networking across the organisation would help here.

Network Connections

Giving thought to a middle managers' own network is helpful. Middle managers exist, obviously, in the middle of organisations. Organisations are themselves networks, and middle managers become a nexus, a hub, within that larger network. It can be a useful exercise to map out this network with middle managers, to uncover who each is connected to, the strength and the appropriateness of these connections. This may lead to realisations for middle managers that they need to be connected to different people.

Middle management can be an isolating experience for many. It does not have to be like that. Having a strong network or community of practice may help provide emotional support for middle managers. Examining the strength of connections with senior leaders would help a middle manager to understand who they are influenced by, and who they in turn influence. If trust helps the interface to be more effective, looking at the network map uncovers where action may be required. The same should be examined for connection strength lower down the hierarchy. Middle managers will be able to see which of their people and teams they may not need to spend as much time explaining strategic direction to, and which of their people and teams may need to have their connection to organisational purpose revisited.

The number of connections a middle manager has in their network is not the same as, but will be influenced by, the span of control and number of direct reports they have. Middle managers with too many direct reports may find it difficult to give each of those the attention and regular check-ins they need, so careful thought should be given to spans of control across the middle management layer. Naturally, different complexities of tasks and functions require different spans, but having some consistency and set of expectations across the organisation would be helpful. A middle manager with only one direct report would struggle to let go of operational responsibility for the team underneath the manager who reports to them – so whilst too many is a bad thing, so might too few be. I would also recommend seeing if there is a correlation between greater spans of control and relative strength (or otherwise) of relationships. There should be. Are you happy with what that shows?

Checking-in

It is hard to specify a frequency or duration for a check-in, other than to say it should be regular enough to have an impact and last long enough to be meaningful for both parties. The expectation to do this should be clearly articulated and written into the role profile of a middle manager. Although it seems like it may be stating the obvious, it serves as a useful reminder of the need for human contact and emotional proximity that can often make the difference in successful middle management. When combined with the right span of control, and leveraging technology (which we discuss below), middle managers will have more energy and time to devote to this important aspect of their role – where they give and receive feedback.

Check-ins should also be regular and meaningful between the middle manager and the senior leader to whom they report. This would enable the middle manager to receive practical feedback and coaching from someone who has been successful in the organisation, something that Training Industry suggests will give a middle manager "a safe place to voice sticky situations" (Training Industry, 2023)

Leveraging Technology

Much of the burden in a middle management position can come from the volume of administrative tasks that need to be completed. Here is where technology, particularly artificial intelligence (AI), can help – by automating mundane, routine tasks, speeding up the gathering of data, and streamlining the decision-making process. This would also free up middle management time to create the human connections, in check-ins, and across their network, which make a difference in their role – to build their social capital. Middle managers should be encouraged and supported to utilise technology in ways that make them more efficient, with the expectation that they do more of the "human" things with the time AI frees up. The middle manager can then spend more time bridging the communication gaps that often exist between senior leadership, and front-line staff.

Bridging Communication Gaps

Middle managers must take conscious, deliberate steps to ensure that the communication gaps that could exist, are either prevented from existing, or minimised. This could involve mobilising different communication methods and techniques, acting as a conduit for two-way feedback up and down the organisation, and contextualising information to aid understanding. The bigger the organisation, the more complicated that can become, and the greater the risk of the communication gap causing issues. The interfaces between senior leadership and middle managers, as mentioned previously in this chapter, are critical to closing the communication gaps, and more so in larger organisations. However, there is a danger that in larger organisations, the nature of senior leadership could make it more introspective and less focused on interfacing with middle management. Middle managers must work hard to manage up and focus on managing down. But how?

Managing Up

The skills required to manage up differ from those required to manage down. Picking the time to share things publicly, and what to share privately, is an understated skill, and middle managers when managing up would be better sharing things privately to protect the more senior leader's reputation and "face." Using emotion appropriately would aid this type of intervention – whilst middle managers are tasked with highly functional or operational targets, they are still human with a full range of emotional reactions, they should let their passions underpin what they do (though not completely control it). When dealing with more senior leaders, preparing in advance is likely to prevent emotional overload, and enable more effective linkage to strategic issues. Feedback should be two-way – as important as it is for the senior leader to hear what the operational teams reporting to the middle manager think, it is equally important for the senior leader to share their feedback and views, and for the middle manager to acknowledge this. Opinions are valuable but are enhanced by use of data and evidence to support decision-making.

The feedback mentioned above could be via a regular update meeting. The senior leader should use the opportunity to clarify what success means for the organisation, and timescales for that. The middle manager could update the senior leader on progress, what the team goals are that are contributing to the wider organisational goals and highlight any issues that may be limiting progress. It could be helpful to document the things discussed and actions agreed too.

But what about managing down?

Managing Down

There is some overlap here even though the direction middle managers are facing is different. Having the ability to plan and see through difficult conversations is an important skill. This requires the ability to utilise a wide range of evidence, to be willing to listen to other (contrary) views, to handle strong emotional content, and to be clear on what takes priority in the organisation. The ability to communicate effectively is a critical skill for managing downwards – knowing what, when, where, why and how to share information, and using judgement rather than gut feel to make such decisions. Enhanced levels of self-awareness, developed through multiple methods, feedback, and insight, will help the middle manager to understand more about the influencing skills and abilities they have, and utilise them appropriately to manage their teams.

Middle managers must be able to see the wider organisational context when managing downwards. Rather than trying to please everyone, they should remind themselves and others of what is happening in the organisation (and why). This can be done through linking individual and team goals to organisational goals and challenging when there is no obvious link to be made. Creating a regular meeting where organisational goals, and team contributions to those, are reviewed, is a helpful step. In that meeting, organisational goals can be discussed to aid understanding and broken down by the middle manager into operational targets and actionable tasks for individuals and the team. The meeting should ensure that all present understand the connection between their work and the organisational goals, as well as its overarching purpose. A useful next step is to discuss obstacles and barriers to achieving the now-broken down goals, and to ask direct reports what help the middle manager could provide in moving forward.

Developing and Supporting Middle Managers to Bridge Communication Gaps

Middle managers are unlikely to achieve these skills by chance. They are also unlikely to thrive at deploying these skills on their own. So, what do we do to increase their chances of success at middle management?

Management is often a very isolating experience, and middle management more so because of its in-between nature. Being a manager can often create the feeling that you are the only person to have the problems and issues that you do, and to instil a sense of fear or shame in admitting that you do not have all the answers. We must work to overcome this.

One useful way would be to create a community of practice for middle managers, where they can come together and talk about being a middle manager. This would allow better sharing of ideas, more effective knowledge management, and provide emotional support for middle managers. Knowing that other middle managers face similar issues may increase the courage and resilience that a middle manager has – they may feel more able to speak up about their issues and concerns. This community of practice would be able to examine what "followership" means in the organisational context – how to effectively manage up – as well as what leadership means – how to effectively manage down.

This should be complemented by a development programme that blends different learning methods and options. We must not assume that all middle managers have the required skills that we have discussed in this chapter and therefore should provide input on all of these and protect the middle managers' time in accessing the available development. It would be useful to engage middle managers themselves in the design of the programme, so that they can share their pain points and frustrations and suggest the right tools and methods which would help them to overcome them. MindTools research found that managers who received access to learning resources, formal courses and training opportunities, particularly at the start of their management career, were significantly better at coaching, goal setting, identifying development opportunities for their people, active listening, and establishing trust (MindTools, 2024). Skilled middle managers, then, because of this development, are better placed to help close those communication gaps.

Closing the Gaps

If the middle manager is engaged with the organisation, they offer some significant benefits to senior leadership. The middle manager may be able to share experiences of implementation of strategy gone well, and where it has failed in the past. They may be able to more easily identify the unique competencies that are within the organisation and their teams and how these lead to competitive advantage, in a way that the more-removed senior leader could not. They will be more able to scan the external environment for threats to that competitive advantage. And if middle managers do these things well, it correlates directly to higher organisational performance (Academy of Management Executive, 2001).

Rachel Wood is the Head of Talent Development at Optimo Care, a health and social care organisation based in the UK and employing around 1,800 staff.

Across Wood's career she has been a middle manager and had responsibility for developing middle managers. In a previous organisation she observed middle management roles being moved into a shared service type of arrangement, enabling them to deliver on strategic priorities but without formally managing anyone. This approach had pros and cons – it did recognise that some middle managers are not suited for the role but also removed their authority whilst retaining their need to influence. The structural change also removed the middle managers from the parts of the business they were supporting but put them close to others in similar positions and created a greater sense of community. Wood's analogy was that this made the middle managers like performance consultants, or a type of business partner. In Wood's own experience this often proved an attractive model for her – she feels that being a middle manager without having responsibility for multiple teams enables her to focus better on what the role requires. She believes that selling middle management to those entering the world of work could be better done by explaining it as a specialist function – the term "middle" implies a squeeze that can be off-putting.

Wood has also seen traditional middle management roles up close. She explained how difficult it is to translate senior management intentions into operational priorities, whilst simultaneously looking after multiple teams AND oneself. In her assessment, only 20% of middle managers do those things well, and sometimes more through luck or trial and error rather than judgement or development. She found that these 20% are more outspoken than others, are excellent communicators, curious, inquisitive, and have lots of relevant life and professional experiences to call upon.

Wood shared her view of what makes a great middle manager:
- People management is a key skill to have but one that Wood believes is too often sidelined in favour of operational issues – middle managers must devote the time to do people management well but often do not (or cannot).
- Wood believes that middle managers must be able to listen well, simplify language and remove jargon, and relate strategic directives to the multiple roles reporting to them. They must be good at asking questions to clarify, and, in Wood's own words, "be confident enough to look like the stupidest person in the room." Wood believes that too many middle managers feel a need to fill silence by talking, but that a better solution is to take time over communication, avoid repetition for its own sake, and let people think during planned silences.
- She believes that the best middle managers are facilitators at heart, and this is backed up by her experience of working alongside many. Expanding on this, she has experienced great middle managers who are storytellers, can control a crowd, and present well. They bring people out of their shells, close distractions, use incisive questioning techniques, and deliver timely and constructive feedback. They are great at spotting and managing team dynamics too.
- Wood believes that middle managers need to know how much time and flexibility is available to them and their teams, and be able to see the pain points and places their attention is needed to

resolve – "what fires need putting out?" – but also be clear on their blind spots, and bits of the organisation that they cannot clearly see.

–   She also believes that relationships are important to cultivate – "its sometimes not what you know, but who you know" – explaining that influencing without authority is best done through one's own social ties and networks within an organisation. Middle managers who only have one or two strong social ties could be isolated if those ties are broken, so Wood recommends a broad spectrum of relationships that are all strong.

In her role, Wood believes she is doing an excellent job if no-one knows she exists. By that she means that she is not obstructing anyone or anything, not getting in anyone's way or being the blocker or bottleneck for anything happening. We discussed whether this could lead to an ignorance of the contribution of middle managers, and concluded that in some organisations, it has. Wood has seen this too, where middle managers are not seen as contributing to output, are cut, and then their presence is swiftly missed. Middle managers, in Wood's view, contribute to outcomes that are often intangible.

Such intangible outcomes are about leveraging their knowledge, experience, and relationships. Middle managers tend to know organisational culture very well, having spent time building trust and being with their teams as well as other parts of the organisation. Wood believes that they have exposure to organisational strategy in a very wide sense, given the breadth of their relationships across the organisation. Senior managers do not have that. First line managers do not have that. The middle management role is unique.

Using Data Better

In this section we will examine how middle managers can make more effective use of data to support their decision-making, improve efficiency, manage risks, and report on team effectiveness and performance. This can be a useful way of bridging the gap between the strategic and the operational since data itself can be a storytelling and communication device. A middle manager, given their position in organisations, will have access to a huge amount of data – about their teams, their individual employees, productivity, and performance, and more besides. Using data (and wider forms of evidence) to make decisions is therefore a way for middle managers to demonstrate their credibility and influence. This relies on those middle managers knowing what data to use for a decision, where to find it, and how to use it. There could be a skill gap, and a mindset issue too because using more than just one's own opinion requires critical thinking. There could be time barriers too, and technological issues to overcome also.

The importance of this cannot be understated. Research from AND Digital revealed 72% of key decision-makers believe that the ability to make decisions using data has become more critical in recent years, but that only 24% of organisations confidently use data to make decisions (Corndel, 2023). McKinsey claims that "by 2025, smart workflows and seamless interactions among humans and machines will likely be as standard as the corporate balance sheet, and most employees will use data to optimise nearly every aspect of their work" (Corndel, 2023).

Some of the skill gaps can be overcome with additional development. Fifty-seven percent of middle managers feel that they do not have sufficient training to do their jobs, affecting their confidence in making decisions and organisational performance (Imutan, 2024). Development could focus on developing data literacy – how to read and interpret patterns and trends in data, some understanding of statistical concepts, and how to draw meaningful conclusions from different data sets (Imutan, 2024). It is my view that many middle managers lack the skills needed to make effective use of data – but that they are not alone in that skill gap. If we can close it, we can unlock the power that middle managers have to transform organisations.

But there is a danger that data overload is reached, that there is too much data to choose from and access. McKinsey report that 60% of middle managers feel overwhelmed by the amount of data they must process daily (Hancock and Field, 2023). This could slow down decision-making rather than improve it. Data analysis tools could help here and could automate some of the analysis, as could practicing the use of decision-making models. However, there is an understated human element that could also help – conversations. The middle manager could have a conversation with their main stakeholders to identify the key data sets that show performance versus organisational goals. They could conduct critical incident analysis to reflect on past situations and identify what data helped – or would have helped – those situations to go better. They could undertake scenario planning with their teams to work out what data would be critical to have in specific situations, and plan how to obtain this in the most efficient way. These crucial conversations may uncover the 20% of data that drives 80% of the decisions middle managers need to make.

The growth of generative AI offers middle managers both opportunities and threats with using data better. AI will easily speed up data collection and analysis and can integrate into decision-making smoothly. But if middle managers struggle with the skills needed to use data, then simply adding AI into the mix will not close the skill gap – it will in many cases widen it. Middle managers struggling with data are also likely to struggle with making effective use of AI and understanding its work correctly. Then, the gaps we have talked about in this chapter could remain and become more misaligned.

Overcoming Misalignment

Misalignment can materialise in many forms. Teams may not trust their middle managers if the communication and explanation of organisational priorities is unclear, or if the goals shared do not appear relevant or achievable to the team. This could lead to wasted resources, and under-performance. But what causes this, and what could be done about it?

The Chartered Management Institute (CMI) found some illuminating statistics in their research into middle management misalignment:

- Only 9% of middle managers are always asked for input or feedback on information provided to them, and 35% are never asked for input or feedback.
- Only 31% of middle managers feel confident communicating company information to their reports, yet 76% say they are expected to communicate and engage their teams with this information.
- 64% of middle managers feel there is a lack of information from the top of the business.
- 65% of middle managers communicate organisational plans and goals with which they do not personally agree. (CMI, 2020)

These are alarming findings. Middle managers want to trust and be trusted by senior leaders, to further develop that trust lower down the organisation. They want to understand organisational goals and priorities better and can challenge and shape them. We have already explained in this chapter that middle managers are crucial to organisational success and play a vital connecting role within organisations. But if middle managers do not feel trusted, and do not trust the senior leaders, then there is a significant risk that all the hopes and plans the organisation has will come to nothing. Middle managers know they are important in building trust, but as the CMI point out, do not have the belief, inspiration, tools, or time to drive strategy delivery (CMI, 2020). Some of the ideas explored in this chapter are helpful for building the necessary trust – regular, frequent check-ins between the middle manager and those who report to them, and between the middle manager and senior leadership. Development pathways and programmes, too, demonstrate commitment and interest in middle managers. We must not leave middle management competency to chance.

Case Studies

Rick Bradley was, at the time we spoke, the Head of Learning and Development (L&D) at WithYou, a charity supporting people affected by substance use and mental health issues. They have around 1,800 staff and volunteers based across the UK. Rick himself is a middle manager, but he and his team support middle managers – the L&D team describe themselves as "the people who support the people who support the people." Middle managers are considered critical to living up to that motto and the L&D team have been doing a lot of work to support them.

Bradley's team are consciously trying to shift the culture within the organisation away from just delivering training as the default option, and their work supporting middle managers is a good example of this as they want to encourage more reflection, more emotional connection, and more practical application of skills and knowledge alongside the "injection education" of the classroom, seeing the blend as important to help middle managers grasp how their unique role could play out. They see middle managers as setting the culture within their areas, and being clear on that cultural role and its impact is a core aspect of the support given to them.

Those new to middle management are given various pieces of support. Firstly, there is a two-day in-person classroom workshop called Core Skills for New Managers. But rather than this focusing on the procedural elements of middle management and the routine work that middle managers are usually tasked with, the workshop focuses on how it feels to be a middle manager. It looks at influence and impact, using a ripple-based sphere of influence and impact activity to map out the middle manager's position and connection with those in their network. This activity is one of the most talked-about and valued by those in attendance and offers immediately practical application. Middle managers are also asked to talk about the impact that their greatest and worst ever managers had on them, and this focuses the middle managers on the emotional impact that a middle manager has on their direct reports and teams.

There are also Action Learning Sets, which are very well-received and encourage peer to peer support and connections, overcoming the sense of isolation that middle managers can often feel. A cultural shift therefore is the development of coaching conversations by middle managers, and less "rescuing" of supervisory managers by middle managers. The Action Learning Sets help to create a psychologically safe culture for middle managers, and Bradley reports honest and open disclosures from participants who often struggle with imposter syndrome and a sense of loss as they move up the organisation. The L&D team believe that supporting middle managers emotionally is critical to their eventual success.

Guidance is also given on the practical side of middle management, some of the more procedural aspects. But this is given via microlearning and provision of templates, toolkits, and checklists, for middle managers to access at the point of need. Where possible, technology is used to automate many of the routine aspects of middle management – a good example being the use of Monday.com to automate project management reporting and updates. Middle managers are given guidance about how to leverage this to best effect, as well as sessions on how to gather and use data better.

Once the new middle manager has completed their initial training, the expectation of growth and development continues. Each middle manager is expected to spend an average of one hour per week on their own personal and professional growth, which is then checked via informal conversations. The middle managers are encouraged to link their own growth to that of their teams, in another cultural shift.

A big focus for Bradley's team is the emotional side of middle management. Bradley reports seeing a lot of emotional fatigue from middle managers. He believes this comes from a lack of role clarity at times, but also from the requirement that middle managers wear multiple hats and balance lots of different responsibilities. The support and guidance are an attempt to mitigate this, but it remains a work in progress. Bradley is conscious that more work could be done to clarify the requirements and expectations of middle management and overcome inconsistencies in how the role plays out but is pleased with the work so far around role modelling behaviours and examining healthy working practices.

Case Study Reflections

In the With You case study, the following points stand out for further reflection:
- Middle managers need guidance, support, and development to be able to undertake the role effectively.
- Sending middle managers on a training course will not on its own equip them for success. Providing a blend and range of learning options and methods is better.
- Encouragement of openness, honesty and vulnerability is helpful in the adjustment that middle managers often must make.
- Middle managers have an emotional and cultural impact on their areas (and by extension the whole organisation) and helping them to map this out and identify how to leverage that positively is helpful.
- Utilising technology and data to support administrative tasks and decision-making is a clever idea, but middle managers will need support on how to do that effectively.
- Setting an expectation of growth and development that middle managers must see through for themselves, and their teams is an effective way to embed that in the culture.
- Organisations must be mindful of the emotional load that middle managers can carry and look for ways to mitigate this.

Action Plan

If you are looking to identify and build the essential skills for thriving middle management, then the following reflection questions should help:
- What methods will you deploy to ensure that middle managers are sufficiently involved in shaping organisational strategy?
- How will you help middle managers to develop the right approach to boundary management?
- How will network mapping aid your understanding of the influence of middle managers?
- What correlation is there between spans of control and influencing ability in your organisation?
- What would regular, frequent check-ins between senior leaders and middle managers look and feel like for you?
- What would regular, frequent check-ins between middle managers and their reports look and feel like for you?
- How can these check-ins be more meaningful for all concerned?
- What technology could free up middle management time to do more tasks requiring a human element?
- How will you develop the necessary skills for managing upwards in middle managers?
- How will you develop the necessary skills for managing downwards in middle managers?
- What would a community of practice for middle managers look and feel like for you?
- What development pathways and methods would work best for middle managers, and why? How will you put these in place?
- What support will you provide to help middle managers make better use of data?

References

CMI (2020) *The Middle Manager Lifeline*. Available at: https://www.managers.org.uk/knowledge-and-insights/research/the-middle-manager-lifeline/

Cole, J. (2021) *It's time to overcome 'middle manager syndrome': Part 1 – training industry*. Available at: https://trainingindustry.com/articles/leadership/its-time-to-overcome-middle-manager-syndrome-part-1/

Corndel (2023) *The frozen middle: The demand for data-driven leadership*. Available at: https://www.corndel.com/news/the-frozen-middle-the-demand-for-data-driven-leadership/

Hancock, B. and Field, E. (2023) *The Future of Middle Management, McKinsey & Company*. Available at: https://www.mckinsey.com/capabilities/people-and-organizational-performance/our-insights/the-future-of-middle-management

Hurt, K. and Dye, D. (2017) *The two leadership skills your middle managers most need – training industry*. Available at: https://trainingindustry.com/articles/leadership/the-two-leadership-skills-your-middle-managers-most-need/

Imutan, J. (2024) *Strategic thinking and decision making: Empowering middle managers for Success, Medium*. Available at: https://jordanimutan.medium.com/strategic-thinking-and-decision-making-empowering-middle-managers-for-success-5c8d0e13cfcb

Jaser, Z. (2021) *The real value of Middle Managers, Harvard Business Review*. Available at: https://hbr.org/2021/06/the-real-value-of-middle-managers

King, A. W., Fowler, S. W., & Zeithaml, C. P. (2001). Managing Organizational Competencies for Competitive Advantage: The Middle-Management Edge. *The Academy of Management Executive (1993–2005), 15*(2), 95–106. Available at: http://www.jstor.org/stable/4165738

MindTools (2024) *Building Better Managers*. Available at: https://www.mindtools.com/thought-leadership/reports/building-better-managers/

Walters, K. (2023) *Shoring up middle managers: Strategies to equip your managers to lead their teams through change and uncertainty*. Available at: https://trainingindustry.com/magazine/summer-2023/shoring-up-middle-managers-strategies-to-equip-your-managers-to-lead-their-teams-through-change-and-uncertainty/

Wooldridge, B. and Floyd, S. (1990) *The strategy process, middle management involvement, and organizational performance – wooldridge – 1990 – strategic management journal – wiley online library*. Available at: https://onlinelibrary.wiley.com/doi/abs/10.1002/smj.4250110305

Chapter Three
Building Leadership In The Middle

Having discussed some of the key leadership issues relevant to middle managers in Chapters 1 and 2, in this chapter we will look at how this could be turned into reality. We will examine the nature of leading from the middle and how that differs from top-down leadership. We will explore the role that emotional intelligence and resilience play in middle management roles. We will briefly touch on how mentoring and coaching can be used as methods to develop such things (noting that Chapter 6 will examine coaching, both done to and done by middle managers, in more detail). And we will examine how middle managers can create a culture of trust, collaboration, and high performance within their areas of responsibility.

Leading From The Middle

It can be difficult to lead from the middle. The oft-conflicting demands of different stakeholders within the organisation come together at middle management level. Senior teams focus on strategic priorities, and front-line teams focus on their daily tasks. External customers and other third parties may focus on quality of product or service. These conflicting demands can lead to "the squeezed middle" effect for middle managers, with consequential impacts on potentially every relevant measure.

Harvard Business Review suggested that 70% of change initiatives fail (HBR, 2005) and the most cited reason for this is breakdown in communication. Middle managers are the hub around which this communication could succeed or fail, so it is vital that they know how to leverage the unique position they are in within organisations. Likewise, middle managers need to have well-developed communication skills as outlined in the previous chapter.

Research has found that middle managers involving their stakeholders in goal setting can increase their engagement and commitment to organisational success (HBR, cited in Imutan, 2024). There are many ways to achieve this alignment and agreement on priorities, which might also improve future collaborative efforts. Some of these could be well-defined techniques such as focus groups, surveys, and meetings. Some could utilise technology, such as Slack, Asana, Monday.com, and MS Teams. All could ensure that differing stakeholder expectations are more clearly communicated and discussed, reducing the likelihood of breakdown in communication or misalignment of goals. This would be particularly true if the

https://doi.org/10.1515/9783111713526-003

middle manager's communication skills emphasise a transparent and honest approach to the dialogue – being open about plans, challenges, and more. According to McKinsey, middle managers spend 30% of their time doing such co-ordinating and aligning tasks (McKinsey, cited in ANC Global, 2024). I would suggest that the more time they spend on such things, the more benefits could be seen.

Middle managers play a critical role in change, innovation, and driving strategic priorities. Mintzberg suggests that 80% of organisational change is led by middle managers (Mintzberg, cited in ANC Global, 2024). I would suggest that this could, and should, be higher – middle managers, through their leadership skills from the middle, should ensure that organisational priorities are contextualised and understood by the front line. They should also be able to clearly articulate issues from the front line to senior teams in a way that is also clearly understood.

Only through deploying effective leadership from the middle can organisations harness the power of middle managers. Only then might barriers be removed, bottlenecks eased, and blockers minimised, enabling organisations to thrive and succeed. Leading in the middle matters. But how is it best done?

Hannah Patchett is currently an HR Business Partner and has worked in HR and L&OD roles. She has experienced being a middle manager but has also had responsibility for developing middle managers at two UK Fire and Rescue services. The organisations have employed between 800 and 1,300 people.

Patchett's own experience, as well as the middle managers she has worked with, evidenced frustrations from working in the squeezed middle. Not being communicated with, or listened to, a lack of autonomy, and difficulties in finding balance where business cases for change are unclear, that keeping teams below top-down directives engaged add additional challenges to business-as-usual challenges. In her view, some senior leaders can lack an understanding or consideration of both the operational and tactical implications of strategic decisions, which prevents middle managers from being able to enable change initiatives in the organisation to succeed. Patchett has also seen senior leaders not fully understand the context that middle managers wrestle with – a good example being dealing with challenging individuals, where senior managers can take a view based on limited data, are unaware of the wider context, or in contrast have empathy for individual issues that contradicts the approach being pursued by the middle manager. Therefore, the senior leader can pressure or impose the middle manager to take a solution that may not be the best course of action in the circumstances (for example, a formal performance management process). The behaviour and approach from senior leaders can prevent middle managers from taking ownership of leading from the middle by either taking away their ability to do so or imposing their own judgement that leading from the middle is overturned or overlooked.

Patchett gave an example of organisational restructures to illustrate some of the inherent conflict that prevents leading from the middle. In one organisation she worked in, senior leaders set the direction of the change and promoted the urgency of it, but did not fully understand what was and was not working on the front line. Middle managers had this insight, but these were not sought from senior leaders, and they were not fully consulted about the changes. As such they were presented with a fait accompli decision to announce to the front line. Patchett's middle managers had a unique position – they could see more of organisations than senior leaders or the front line could and could therefore access and influence a wider stakeholder base. This could enable them to start gathering positive sentiment and support the change within organisations – which can be a double-edged sword. In the restructure example, middle managers could have challenged misinformation and managed communication channels but were not given the autonomy to do either. Senior leaders failed to tap into knowledge that middle managers had about their teams, their personalities, and the micro-cultures that could make-or-break the restructure/change initiative. Middle managers looked foolish and ill-prepared for not being privy to senior leadership discussions and decisions and did not feel fully connected to the top or bottom of the organisation. They could not lead from the middle.

Patchett shared her views about how middle managers can display leadership from the middle:

– Define the role. Patchett's experience is that middle management is ill-defined, with vague expectations and requirements that are too different from the tier below them. The jump to middle management is therefore akin to a leap into the unknown, and for some this can feel like a 'sink or swim' scenario.

– Prepare them for it. Middle management is a different ask than supervisory management, where such managers can often "go native" in Patchett's experience. Middle managers are by their very nature more corporate, but a lack of exposure to such environments for front-line staff can often be problematic for unprepared new middle managers, and Patchett has seen many crumbles at losing what engaged them as a supervisory manager. Patchett recommends support (as outlined below) but also offering aspiring middle managers the opportunity to "act up" into vacant middle manager positions for a temporary period, allowing them and the organisation to assess fit and skill gaps. If there are no vacant positions, Patchett has been able to arrange project management opportunities instead, and the ability to work alongside those operating well at that middle management level.

– Develop them right. Patchett has not yet encountered a consistently successful development method for middle managers and recommends a range of methods to provide an offer that suits different learning styles and development needs. She believes formal workshops and training are not the start and end of middle management development options, and recommends coaching, mentoring, and peer-to-peer support to supplement formal, standardised development programmes. She recommends an equal focus on both leadership, and management, recognising the unique position of middle managers who usually need to focus on both simultaneously.

– Support them from the top. Senior leaders need to take an active role in developing and supporting middle managers, and Patchett recommends a semi-formal process where senior leaders and middle managers regularly meet and reflect on how the middle management experience has been. Regular communication between the groups can identify what is and is not working and reduce tension between the two groups.

– Encourage overcommunication. Patchett has seen problems caused when middle managers under-communicate or adopt an inconsistent approach to communication. She advises guiding middle managers on how to utilise multiple communication channels, how to be inclusive in communications, and to build a communication depository to support middle managers in being more consistent in communication.

Leading Laterally – Influencing Without Authority

Many middle managers need to leverage their positions better. This involves leading not up or down (though both happen) but across the organisation and influencing those over whom they have no authority. This can be difficult.

Harvard Business School propose three main ways to influence without authority:

– Through expertise – being recognised for having a unique skillset or knowledge base that few, if any, others in the organisation possess – consequently, others in the organisation are likely to listen to the middle manager when they speak.

– Through relationships – recognising that knowledge alone is not enough and using the strength of one's own social capital to get things done. Harvard explain this as people being more inclined to listen to the middle manager if they believe that they are talking to a person, not just a coworker, and if they believe the middle manager would do the same for them given the opportunity.

– Through understanding the business – a deep understanding of how decisions are made, how business processes operate, and how other functions work (HBS, 2019).

Harnessing these ways of influencing will enhance the middle managers ability to lead from the middle. The middle manager will have some authority that comes with their position but having high emotional intelligence (which we expand upon later in this chapter), a low ego and a general willingness to listen to and learn from others will be important to develop.

French and Raven's Power Bases model is a helpful way for middle managers to understand where influence comes from within an organisation, and how they might better leverage the attributes they already have – or work to develop them:

– Legitimate power – the position a person holds within the organisation and the power that flows from that position.

– Reward power – the ability to compensate someone for doing something.

– Expert power – based on a person's elevated level of skill or knowledge.

– Referent power – the result of perceived attractiveness, worthiness or right to respect.

– Coercive power – the ability to punish someone for not doing something.

– Informational power – the ability to control access to information that others need (French and Raven, 1959)

Building an understanding of the middle management power base for individual middle managers and the collective tier of middle managers will uncover whether anything needs to change within the organisation to improve how middle managers manage up and manage down.

Balancing Managing Up With Managing Down

Gjerde and Alveson neatly summarise the balancing act that a middle manager must undertake: "both their subordinates and superiors may very well be present in the same room, interact or become privy to the messages that are conveyed to the other group. This renders the task more daunting, as discrepancies or inconsistencies in their messages may easily be identified and potentially undermine their authority and credibility" (Gjerde and Alveson, 2024). This highlights the dexterity needed of middle managers who must face in opposing directions simultaneously, or at least consecutively. It could be dizzying to continually shift perspectives in such a way. No wonder balancing managing up and managing down is tricky, and it can be challenging for the middle manager to be authentic in such situations. Gjerde and Alveson highlight the risk that a middle manager may resort to "role distancing" because of this, consciously done to manage the impressions that their audience at the time may have of middle management – but with consequential damage to authenticity (Gjerde and Alveson, 2024).

Role distancing may enable a middle manager to present a more "acceptable" face to the specific audience (e.g. senior leaders, or front line staff) and maintain an element of popularity with both separately, but is a form of acting, and not necessarily the best use of the middle management position. Rather, the middle manager should act as a middle manager, not as other audiences may like to see middle managers. Authenticity, consistency, and reliability all matter in middle management roles, but are often underplayed.

A middle manager is likely to wear multiple hats. As a minimum they will be a functional expert and a middle manager, spending time doing what comes with each role. They need to be consciously aware when to metaphorically take off one hat and put on the other. There is a right time, and a wrong time, for each hat to be worn. I would suggest that wearing the middle management hat is often underplayed and underutilised by many middle managers, to maintain smooth relationships with all stakeholders. But it should not be. Middle managers must BE middle managers when managing up and managing down.

Wayne Ledden is a Contact Centre Manager at Yes Insurance, an insurance provider based in Ireland. He spoke to me about his time at both that organisation and a previous organisation, also an insurance provider, as a middle manager.

Ledden did not want to be a middle manager but was encouraged within the organisations to grow and develop. He became interested in developing people and services and found that middle management allowed for both – although this was not clearly outlined before he got into the role. Ledden wanted to help people to grow, to build relationships, and to be involved in change and improvement activities – things that only a middle management position could provide for him.

In his current position, Ledden must both manage up and across the business in ways that he had not previously done. He was helped with the role being brand new – no-one had done it previously, allowing Ledden some scope in building it. His focus has been to build teams, services, and processes – and did this swiftly, recruiting lots of people in a brief time. Because of the fast-paced growth and change in the business, Ledden has had to give his teams autonomy – he has recruited them because they have the right skills and sees his role as giving them the space to use those skills and make the right decisions. He is far from a micro-manager, and is transparent and open in his approach, sharing information widely amongst the teams.

Ledden, in the new role, provided Yes with something different as a middle manager. They had been used to "old school" middle managers, but Ledden was consciously acting differently. He sees middle management as being part of and leading conversations and helping teams to be their best – not just passing communication up and down the organisation. He set the blueprint for what middle managers should be at Yes.

When managing up, Ledden makes sure he understands the unique styles that senior leaders have, and how they lead and communicate. He ensures that there are shared expectations about how he will work with them. When managing across the organisation, Ledden uses other middle managers as peer-to-peer coaches and a community of practice to get the support he needs. He finds joint working and socialisation opportunities to influence better. And when managing down, he ensures that his teams have a good understanding of how each of the other teams work without having to work in the same way. He works with the teams to develop shared understanding of goals and values, and strong interfaces between them.

In the above example, we see how a middle manager, when given freedom to operate, can achieve the right levels of influence and the right style of managing.

When managing up, consider how to bring solutions and not problems to the senior team. The middle manager can often be seen to be "going native" if they simply repeat what their teams have told them. Whilst the issues are real, the senior teams are likely to have more time and respect for the middle manager who comes with options, recommendations, and potential solutions for the senior team to debate and decide upon.

When managing down, consider how to be clearer on organisational priorities and decision-making processes to the front-line teams. The middle manager could be seen to be "a corporate poodle" if they simply repeat what senior teams have told them. Whilst those things need communicating, they need doing in a way that respects the organisational priorities but breaks them down into tangible actions that front line teams can understand. The front-line teams are likely to have more time and respect for the middle manager who comes to them not just with the big picture, but with the project plan and engagement activities that create buy-in, and who listens to their ideas and input. But what are the skills needed to do these things?

Critical Leadership Skills to Develop in Middle Managers

In most chapters in this book we touch on the key skills needed for success in middle management positions. There is some deliberate repetition, as well as some building on earlier themes, here. Middle managers need development, and this point is reinforced with each passing chapter. Some of the skills they need they will have gained in previous roles, but by no means all. Some skills are of greater importance in a middle management position though, since that layer need to possess all the technical skills from previous roles and add to them with various relevant "soft" skills that are crucial for middle management.

We exist in a technologically enabled world and work more so is affected by the rise of artificial intelligence taking the weight of some of our responsibilities. Middle management could feel threatened by that but should not. Whilst artificial intelligence could replace some middle management functions, it will not replace many of the human elements that middle management do better than most – or where middle management can demonstrate most of their impact. Things like feedback, leadership, mentoring, coaching, empathy, connection, networking, influencing, and much more. However, Accenture found in 2019 that 77% of leaders had significant weaknesses in those types of skills (Accenture, cited in Coach-Hub, n.d.). It is highly likely that the dial has not shifted much, or at all since that research. Development can significantly help middle managers, and yet much of what organisations currently provide focuses on processes, systems, products, services, and compliance – not leadership. But if done right, the evidence suggests a strong correlation between skilled middle managers and successful business outcomes:

- Harvard Business Review showed that companies with strong middle management report up to 15% higher financial performance.
- The same study showed that 70% of organisational success hinges on middle management.
- McKinsey showed that 85% of companies with effective middle management experienced higher performance metrics, and a 20% increase in productivity.

- Google's Project Oxygen explored the traits of top-performing managers and found that those middle managers with such traits saw an increase in team performance by 75%.
- The American Journal of Sociology found that organisations with robust middle management exhibit higher levels of employee satisfaction, and lower turnover. (C-Suite Strategy, 2024)

And yet, we know from Chapter 1 that many middle managers feel disengaged or burnt out. Forbes suggest that only 29% of middle managers feel satisfied with the development opportunities provided by their organisations (Forbes, cited in C-Suite Strategy, 2024). Middle managers do not feel supported, but if they did – through development opportunities, mentoring, coaching, and peer support – they are likely to be higher performing and more engaged. We must do better, but at what, and how?

Emotional Intelligence (Ei)

There are a number of good reasons why EI is increasingly important for middle managers. With the growth of dispersed teams and digital communication, EI comes to the fore – Forbes suggest that 85% of successful middle managers exhibit elevated levels of EI, enabling them to better connect with their teams, resolve conflict and foster collaboration (C-Suite Strategy, 2024). With teams becoming increasingly diverse, EI will help middle managers keep them engaged and productive. However, most traditional management development programmes do not consciously emphasise the importance of EI, focusing instead on process- and task-driven capabilities instead (such as delegation, time management, goal setting, and more).

Examples of EI-type qualities that middle managers should be developed in include:
- Empathy – an understanding of what individuals and teams need.
- Effective communication – the ability to clearly articulate one's own and other people's ideas.
- Self-awareness – being aware of the impact that one's own behaviour has on others.
- Social skills – being able to network with others and build new relationships.
- Adaptability – being able to respond well to new situations and environments and recover from setbacks.
- Learning from criticism – seeing feedback and criticism as an opportunity for growth and reflection, rather than a personal attack

–   Influencing – having the ability to positively affect the thinking and actions of others (adapted from Masters in Minds, 2024).

We could also reinforce the importance of EI by building it into how middle managers performance is assessed – for example how they actively demonstrate such qualities. Sometimes these qualities come naturally, but they can be developed with the right effort.

Change Management and Communication Skills

Middle managers, as we have examined, play critical roles in communicating and implementing change. Middle managers themselves may be resistant to change but we must not underestimate the impact that they can have on organisational change effectiveness. They can be resistant to change because the status quo may have got them to the position they are in, and they could feel under threat from any change to accepted cultural norms or established practices (Globe and Mail, 2017). But the impact they could have is stark – we mentioned that 70% of change initiatives are deemed to fail, but Harvard Business Review suggests that if middle managers are engaged and empowered around change management, and skilled at it, their teams are five times more likely to achieve successful transformations (C-Suite Strategy, 2024).

If the change is around technology, then middle managers will need to understand the digital advances being introduced, but more importantly be able to ensure its smooth adoption within their teams, and to guide their teams towards the shared goal. Communication, problem-solving, and decision-making skills, will be crucial in this – change management is rarely about the what or the when, but about the who and the why.

We must develop middle managers to be excellent communicators who can relay information up and down the organisation to aid change initiatives. We must develop them to be great coaches who can work with individuals to identify blockers and generate commitment to change. We must develop them to be adaptable – focusing on business-as-usual at times and knowing when to focus on change programmes at others. We must develop their ability to multi-task effectively, using project and time management tools to be more organised and leveraging technology to ensure things stay on target.

Middle managers must be skilled at critical thinking, incisive questioning, and active listening. They will need to be good at interpreting and passing on data and feedback. This will enable them to handle the potentially enormous amounts of information they need to process, and to more effectively liaise with stakeholders. They will need to be capable of accessing and using a range of influencing styles to get stuff done. They are the hub around which social and information exchanges take place. We must ensure they are given the appropriate development and support to be able to do these things well.

Bridges' Transition Model is a helpful one to explore here with middle managers. Bridges neatly summarises what middle managers need to do at three distinct stages of change – endings, the neutral zone, and beginnings. This could be used as a checklist of things that middle managers need to become competent in – from acknowledging and respecting losses, permitting people to express anger or sadness, protecting people from unnecessary changes, being realistic on output expectations, ensure people understand their role in the change's outcome, and modelling the attitudes and behaviours they expect of others (Bridges, 1991).

Resilience

Much of middle management is about pressure, about reconciling different forces. This could easily cause stress in middle managers, so they must develop resilience. This would help them to handle stress, uncertainty, and tricky situations better – keeping their focus on what is important whilst maintaining their own health. What separates great middle managers from the rest is the ability to adjust, adapt, respond and be resourceful in the face of all of this (CCL, 2020). To do that, a good start point would be to help middle managers understand themselves better – their preferences, their style, their strengths. They can then be encouraged to understand their teams better in the same ways – and help those teams to focus on their own health and resilience too.

Some middle managers may be plainly not cut out for the role. Professor Cary Cooper, cited in a CIPD podcast, believes that 20% of people are excellent managers and should stay as such; 60% could get there with some training and coaching and mentoring; and 20% should not go near managing people at all (CIPD, 2023). He goes on to explain that bad managers are bad not just for their own health, but for other people's health also. In the same podcast, Amanda Arrowsmith likens most organisational approaches to developing managers as like learning to drive. We pass our driving test and are then assumed to be able to drive competently for decades (CIPD, 2023) despite clear advances in technology, safety guidance, and more. Yet we assume that managers, once promoted into the role and given some initial development, would be fine for a similar period. By sheer chance, they might be. But is that the kind of thing you want to leave to chance? Culturally, we may be resistant to tackling this – but tackle it we must. If we wish to have a high-performance culture, we must lay the groundwork for this by developing middle managers to create and nurture it.

High-Performance Cultures and Middle Managers

A high-performance culture is an important one to develop if a middle manager is going to demonstrate their impact by leading from the middle. It is something that should permeate throughout the organisation as it reflects a collective mindset that is built upon collaboration, accountability, a drive for excellence, and a commitment to learning and growth (People Management, 2023). But whilst this might be considered to flow from the top of an organisation, it is in it's middle that it becomes more than aspirational, more than words on a page. Middle managers are central to its creation.

We have discussed how middle managers are critical in doing specific things that contribute to a high-performance culture, including (but not limited to):

– Communicating organisational goals in a way that should motivate their teams to perform to meet them. This is done by clarifying purpose – how individual and team priorities contribute to organisational priorities, and how the organisational priorities are reflected in individual and team operations and practices.
– Connecting employees to the work of other teams and the wider organisation so that those employees feel they are part of a bigger picture. Storytelling is a key aspect of this, particularly where change is concerned.
– Encouraging their teams to grow, giving them opportunities to expand their knowledge and skills base in the face of sometimes rapidly changing circumstances that require agility and adaptability at work.
– Promoting team development and team building activities that promote collaboration, and connecting the team to the work of other organisational teams
– Providing feedback to teams on their performance against agreed goals and reducing blockages to progress through leveraging relationships with stakeholders across the business.
– Role modelling organisational values and the behaviours they expect from their teams and challenging those both within their teams and across the organisation who do not do the same. Employees take cues from the signals emitted by middle managers. If middle managers can showcase the values and behaviours that deliver the greatest value and success to the organisation, employees are likely to follow suit.

McKinsey research shows that organisations with high-performance cultures create a 3x return to shareholders (McKinsey, 2018), which highlights the importance of showing middle managers how to create this. There is more to it than just frequently repeating messages from senior leaders on purpose, values and more. For it to work, middle managers must be trusted, and employees must collaborate with them and with each other.

Trust in Middle Managers

Trust matters in both life and work. Strategic goals set by an organisation cannot be fully achieved without employees trusting the senior leaders who set such goals. And that trust flows through middle managers in both directions. Without trust in middle managers, strategic goals could be threatened. But often middle managers lack the skills or insight needed to create trust, and become bottlenecks in information sharing, or unconsciously filter out important perspectives. When that happens, employees feel disconnected from strategic direction, potentially disengaged in their work, and distrustful of their middle managers. We must avoid this. We are, in general, failing to avoid it. Research by the Chartered Management Institute (CMI) found that only 36% of middle managers trusted their senior leaders – contrasting with 72% of senior leaders believing that their middle managers trusted them! And only 31% of middle managers felt confident to communicate senior leaders' intentions to their teams (HR Magazine, 2016). This could be addressed by creating meaningful opportunities for middle managers to quiz – and not just hear – senior leaders, where decision-making is discussed in a transparent and open way, and where the senior leaders visibly prioritise the importance of such exchanges. These opportunities address how middle managers can build trust with the senior team but also vice versa. Middle managers need to be able to share what is working and what is not with senior leaders and collaborate with them to determine what messages to share with their teams – why, and how. These could be done via joint events, where senior leaders and middle managers can connect in a well-planned structure, both formally and informally.

CMI research suggested that for middle managers to trust senior leaders, the three most important things senior leaders need to do are:
– Reveal their thinking on critical issues
– Admit their mistakes
– Encourage middle managers to raise issues (CMI, 2016)

We have talked already in this chapter about the need for middle managers to have first class communication skills. These are crucial for beginning to build trust. If middle managers can display active listening, incisive questioning, and know how to tailor information to different audiences then their teams may listen more intently to them. If there are multiple channels for two-way communication, then their teams may begin to use them if they believe the middle managers will pay more than just lip-service to them. But it is more than about communication. There are other things that middle managers can do to improve trust with their teams:

- Empower. Give their managers teams as much flexibility and autonomy as possible to work how they determine is best for the task at hand.
- Give space. A middle manager should not micromanage any manager reporting to them, or their teams. Middle managers should let go of many operational tasks and trust their reports to manage those, enabling the middle manager to focus on cross-organisational and more strategic matters.
- Show vulnerability. Middle managers should show that they are human and demonstrate humility. They should recognise that they do not – and don't have to – know more about the work of the team than the team themselves, and they aren't – and don't have to be – better at managing that team than its own manager. Instead, middle managers should regularly reinforce how others are better placed to solve problems and generate solutions. Being open and authentic in this way can enhance social ties and relationships with reports.
- Enabling and not blocking work. Middle managers can often be bottlenecks in decision-making, slowing work down and causing frustration and delay. Becoming aware of that gives an opportunity to revisit where, how, and by whom, decisions can be made more effectively. It may also open discussions about where the middle manager could devote energy to reducing blockers to work elsewhere in the organisation. Teams will gain trust through seeing the middle manager devoted to enabling work.
- Being reliable. Consistency and reliability are effective ways of generating trust. If a middle manager can be relied upon to act, behave, and make decisions in a consistent way, that can build trust. This would be even more pronounced if these were in line with espoused organisational and personal values.
- Sharing good practice and mistakes. No middle manager exists in a vacuum, and they must consciously seek out and share good practice from both within and outside the organisation with their teams. It should not all be about sharing what is good. Sharing mistakes, particularly their own, and the learning they got from that mistake, is likely to strengthen relationships with their teams.

–	Being human. Middle managers are just as human as everyone else and finding the time and space to act and be human at work is important in building connection and therefore trust. If their reports and teams know that the middle manager cares for them as individuals and collectively, and is capable of warmth, this could increase their faith in that middle manager.

Case Studies

Adrian Emmott is a Leadership and Performance Coach at Yorkshire Water, a utilities company based in the North of the UK, employing around 5,000 people. Emmott spoke with me about Yorkshire Water's People Leader Pathway, an 11 month learning journey which Emmott and his colleagues designed and deliver to first- and second-line managers within the organisation.

When Emmott arrived at Yorkshire Water there were no formal development in place for middle managers, with most things left to individuals to organise themselves. He felt that most middle managers had gained that role by being good at the job underneath, and noticed many struggles with delegation, letting go of operational responsibilities, and very reactive behaviour based on operational requirements. He believed that there were too many managers but too few leaders in that tier, and that few had had exposure to positive role models to learn from.

The new People Leader Pathway was designed to show middle managers (and others able to access the Pathway) where leaders should be in Yorkshire Water, and to bring that to life. It focused on the roles and responsibilities of people leaders, based on the employee lifecycle, and drawing distinctions (and examining any overlap) between leadership, and management, by focusing on the behaviours of each. The Pathway was popular and got immediate signoff within the organisation, as it was based on tackling several measures – low engagement, inconsistent levels of performance, and high turnover.

The Pathway introduced lots of different learning methods where previously learning was restricted to formal classroom settings. Emmott consciously followed the 70–20–10 model, and included virtual classrooms, face to face classrooms, individual coaching, group coaching, strengths-based psychometric testing, and peer to peer support. The Pathway was not mandated, but Yorkshire Water strongly encouraged middle managers to go through it either through direct invites or nominations from senior leaders.

At the time we spoke, nearly 200 middle managers had completed or were completing the Pathway (across fourteen different cohorts) with a retention rate of 85% within the programme. Noting the impact, Emmott and his colleagues built two other Pathways to run alongside the original – an Aspiring Colleague

Pathway (designed for future leaders and for project managers); and a Strategic Leader Pathway (for current and future senior leaders).

The content of the People Leader Pathway is based on organisational competencies, behaviours, and strategic vision, ensuring that middle managers can effectively lead from the middle on such things. The focus is on ensuring that middle managers understand organisational strategy and why decisions are made, and on managing across the organisation just as much as managing up or down it. Content, delivered in multiple ways, includes:

- The role and responsibilities of People Leaders
- Talking performance at Yorkshire Water
- Ideal Self
- Radical Candour and Coaching
- Leading Change and Resilience
- Performance Excellence
- Engaging and Influencing Others
- Trust in High-Performance Teams
- Adaptive Leadership
- Mentoring (because there is an expectation that around half of the Pathway participants then actively mentor someone on the Aspiring Colleague Pathway)

I also asked Emmott how the Pathway and its work has been evaluated – what difference is it making within Yorkshire Water? He explained that the emphasis is on the performance and behaviour of both leaders and their direct reports, and that his team have evaluated the difference between those measures for Pathway participants vs those middle managers who did not participate using key drivers in the six-monthly organisation engagement survey. The overall conclusion is that those who have been through the Pathway are better leaders. Specific data gathered included:

- Direct reports of the leaders on the Pathway are deemed to be performing better in role by their leaders than other Yorkshire Water employees
- Direct report scores increased in all ten key organisational leadership metrics from survey to survey
- Overall engagement in direct reports of leaders on the Pathway is increasing at a rate higher than and overtaking all Yorkshire Water

Case study refletions

In the Yorkshire Water case study, the following points stand out for further reflection:

- There are always opportunities to improve middle managers, even if the culture has been not to focus on them previously
- Clarifying the distinct leadership, and management, responsibilities of middle managers is helpful in understanding the role better
- Development options should not be limited to formal classroom-based activities, and a wider range of methods is useful
- Agreeing how the development will be evaluated before beginning it gives a good benchmark to later evaluate its impact – and there are multiple measures to examine
- Linking development content to organisational values and competencies helps to embed the development in organisational reality
- Considering the place of development for middle managers in the wider learning ecosystem alongside other development routes for other parts of the organisation means that it is neither an add-on nor a nice-to-have
- Evaluating using control groups shows the impact in greater depth

Action plan

If you want to help your middle managers lead more effectively from the middle, then you could consider how to answer the following questions:
- How many of your change initiatives fail to achieve their aims, and what can middle managers do about that?
- How will you encourage your middle managers to involve stakeholders in goal setting?
- What are the bases of middle management influence, and how will you maximise their effect?
- What will you do to minimise "role distancing" by middle managers?
- How will you develop your middle managers confidence in using technology to lead?
- What can be done to raise awareness of the level of Emotional Intelligence that middle managers have, and then to raise the levels they have?
- How can middle managers communication skills be raised to aid with effective change management?
- How can you encourage middle managers to lead more effectively through transitions?
- What will you do to raise levels of self-awareness amongst middle managers?
- How will you encourage middle managers to develop a high-performance culture with and within their teams?

- What methods would help develop trust between middle managers and senior leaders?
- What methods would help develop trust between middle managers and their teams?

References

ANC Global (2024) *Why middle managers are your organization's make or break.* Available at: https://www.linkedin.com/pulse/why-middle-managers-your-organizations-make-break-ancglobalhr-ivwpe/

Bridges, W (1991) *Bridges transition model.* Available at: https://wmbridges.com/about/what-is-transition/

CCL (2024) *The leadership skills that managers in the middle need to advance.* Available at: https://www.ccl.org/articles/leading-effectively-articles/6-skills-middle-level-leaders-need/

CIPD (2023) *Are people managers doing too much, or not enough?* Available at: https://www.cipd.org/uk/knowledge/podcasts/role_modern_people_manager/

CMI (2016) *The Middle Manager Lifeline.* Available at: https://www.managers.org.uk/knowledge-and-insights/research/the-middle-manager-lifeline/

CoachHub (2023) *Manager in the middle: The challenges and opportunities of Middle Management.* Available at: https://www.coachhub.com/en/blog/manager-in-the-middle-the-challenges-and-opportunities-of-middle-management/

Dewar, C. and Doucette, R. (2018) *6 elements to create a high-performing culture*, McKinsey & Company. Available at: https://www.mckinsey.com/capabilities/people-and-organizational-performance/our-insights/the-organization-blog/6-elements-to-create-a-high-performing-culture

Fitzgerald, R. (2024) *The dynamic role of Middle Management in modern organizations*, C-Suite Strategy. Available at: https://www.c-suite-strategy.com/blog/the-dynamic-role-of-middle-management-in-modern-organizations

Gjerde, S. and Alvesson, M. (2025), *Living the Janus Face: The Promise and Perils of Role-Distancing for Middle Managers. Journal of Management Studies, 62*: 29–64. Available at: https://doi.org/10.1111/joms.13041

Imutan, J. (2024) *Bridging the gap: Building and maintaining stakeholder relationships in middle management.* Available at: https://jordanimutan.medium.com/bridging-the-gap-building-and-maintaining-stakeholder-relationships-in-middle-management-d6c176feda24

McCann, S. (2024) *Case Study – Leaders with high emotional intelligence, Masters in Mind.* Available at: https://www.mastersinminds.com/case-study.-leaders-with-high-emotional-intelligence—blog-1

Mackenzie, D. (2023) *How to cultivate a high-performance culture.* Available at: https://www.peoplemanagement.co.uk/article/1839814/cultivate-high-performance-culture

Miller, K (2019) *How to influence without authority in the workplace*, Business Insights Blog. Available at: https://online.hbs.edu/blog/post/influence-without-authority

Reynolds, J. (2017) *What is the frozen middle, and why should it keep leaders up at night?*, The Globe and Mail. Available at: https://www.theglobeandmail.com/report-on-business/careers/leadership-lab/what-is-the-frozen-middle-and-why-should-it-keep-leaders-up-at-night/article34862887/

Sirkin, H.L., Keenan, P. and Jackson, A. (2005) *The hard side of Change Management, Harvard Business Review.* Available at: https://hbr.org/2005/10/the-hard-side-of-change-management

Woodman, P. (2024) *Boosting trust in your middle managers*, HR Magazine. Available at: https://www.hrmagazine.co.uk/content/features/boosting-trust-in-your-middle-managers

Chapter Four
Leading In Transition – Embracing Change

Several times already in this book we have touched on the crucial role that middle managers play in organisations. This is obvious when one comes to examine organisational change. As we have discussed, change within organisations can become something of a constant, but around two-thirds of organisational changes fail to achieve their aims. There is therefore something that middle managers are not able to do, or failing to do, and there is much they can do to rectify this. In this chapter we'll explore the role of middle managers in driving organisational change, how they can manage resistance to change, maintain morale, and align teams behind changed organisational goals. We will also look at tools and frameworks that could help the middle manager to do these things more effectively.

The Role of Middle Management in Organisational Change

Middle managers play a critical role. They are, by virtue of their position, the liaison or middle person between senior leadership and front-line employees in communicating the change vision and then bringing it to life. They may take the brunt of both resistance to the change from the front line, and frustration from senior leadership about lack of progress with the change. All this whilst maintaining performance and dealing with the effects of change on their own roles. It is a unique blend of various levels of involvement in change, not replicated anywhere else in organisational life.

We can usually notice specific roles being played in organisational change and how each contributes to the hoped-for success of said change. Some of these could be done by middle management:

- Change manager – like a project manager but focusing on the human side of change. Change, as you will know, is often not about the what, or the when, but about the why, and the who. An effective change manager will use change tools and methodologies to run alongside project management tools and methodologies to leverage success. If the middle manager is also the change manager, they can utilise their position to ensure that stakeholders are adequately involved and informed, and that communication flows well up, down, and across the organisation.
- Change sponsor – this will usually be a senior leader, but in large organisations it could be a middle manager. They provide commitment from the organisation itself that the change is important and utilise their influence and au-

https://doi.org/10.1515/9783111713526-004

thority to remove barriers to the change. They may also be instrumental in building a guiding coalition for the change. If this is a middle manager, again their unique position within the organisation affords them access to a wider range of stakeholders to achieve these things and increases their ability to be visible throughout the change.

Aside from these roles, which may or may not be filled by a middle manager, there are other roles that will be:
- People managers – managing those who manage front line teams who are affected by the change. This role involves a large degree of communication and coaching, of explaining change, and supporting teams in working through their issues. Middle managers fill this role whether they want to or not.
- Change champions – promoting the change using proactive support to those affected, amplifying communication of the change, providing training, and role modelling the change behaviours that are required. Middle managers again fill this role whether they want to or not.
- HR/OD/L&D professionals – some of these will be middle managers themselves but regardless can act as a supportive partner to middle managers during times of change, helping them manage the emotional and practical challenges that come with change.

The above roles highlight some of the key aspects of change management, and where middle managers can make or break the organisational change.

Middle managers will often find out about organisational changes before their front-line teams and managers, and usually directly from senior leaders. These senior leaders will have been aware of the need to change for some time and will usually have grappled with the pros and cons of it before informing middle managers. This can result in some frustration from senior leaders, who are ready to change, whilst the middle managers do their own grappling with that change. Middle managers must be given time to interpret the change, and to discuss it directly with senior leaders. Middle managers need to make sense of how the change impact them as individuals, but also process how it might shift their priorities, power, and responsibilities before involving their reports (Hirsch, 2022).

This interpretation is best done in two ways. Middle managers should be able to connect with peers – each other – to do this processing, to talk amongst themselves and discuss what pushback might be appropriate. This isn't troublemaking, but a natural reaction to change, and something that senior leaders should appreciate as they are likely to have gone through similar reactions themselves, albeit at an earlier stage in the change process. The other way is for middle managers to do some of this processing directly with senior leaders, ensuring that their interpretation of organisational culture is accurate.

Diane Allton progressed to being a middle manager in a UK-based charitable organisation. As soon as she took on the role, she needed to merge two teams together and handle redundancies and restructures. She found that some of the teams did not understand the need for change, and that she had to lead it without having been involved in the decision-making.

Allton felt that she, and other middle managers in similar situations, were left to figure out how to implement the change with minimal guidance from above. Allton decided to research and source her own training and support and found some that covered how to support teams through change, how to focus on relationships and keep team engagement as high as possible. She benefitted from learning alongside others from different organisations, and the cohort became a useful community of practice. Allton left the course feeling she could focus more on building a team who were more inclusive and listening with attention to each other.

Allton set up a weekly 30-minute virtual meeting for her team, which initially met with a little reluctance from some – the team were not sure they had the time to attend. However, Allton persisted, and ran these meetings with a focus on how the team were feeling, sharing information across the team, storyboarding the change process, and being human with each other. These were supplemented with frequent one to one meetings with each person in the team.

Allton and her team became responsible for supporting others through change, with resources and scheduled workshops. Lots of other teams had to go through organisational restructures and often middle managers lacked clarity about these changes. They were not able to share much useful information or context, or help their teams understand and work through it. Allton's team began ensuring that they could actively support those teams and help them through their own changes, using similar approaches that Allton had learnt from her own external training.

Allton sometimes felt lonely as a middle manager within the organisation. She had responsibility to lead the change, but sometimes lacked the support to do that. She believes that middle managers need to have a strong organisational network, and she sourced her own coach and mentor to help provide the guidance and support needed.

In the example above, we see how middle managers can make a difference in change processes, but only if the rest of the organisational ecosystem allows them to., Middle managers need to know who their backers/supporters are and who they might not be. In her isolated position, Allton didn't have the strength of network that she would have liked, and this contributed to her sense of frustration with what was happening in the organisation during its changes – she wasn't able to influence the way she believes a middle manager can, or should.

Genuine two-way communication between senior leaders and middle managers achieves several things. Senior leaders are unlikely to be able to fully see the impact of major organisational changes on the day-to-day tasks carried out by front line employees. But middle managers should and could explain that to senior leaders. Middle managers can also help to position major organisational changes in the context of other things going on for their reports, and to raise anything that may get in the way of the major change with senior leaders. Having this type of discussion could lead to barriers being minimised, or senior leaders gaining a greater level of patience whilst middle managers and their reports work through the processing of the change. It could also result in middle managers being given more responsibility or autonomy for making decisions about the change

Giving middle managers some involvement in the planning and implementation of the change would also harness their ability to make sense of organisational matters – "middle managers influence organizational processes by navigating complexities and ambiguities. Their role as mediators between executives and front-line employees shapes organizational continuity and change" (Winston et al, 2023). Sense-making is an under-appreciated and under-utilised ability that middle managers have during times of major organisational change. Sense-making allows middle managers to give consideration to the impact of change on a social and collaborative level for their reports and teams. Change may still be top down, but it will be a more considered approach, with tailored communication and engagement approaches because the change has been made to make sense by middle managers. This involvement allows middle managers to be more on board with the organisational change, and to more effectively support it and their teams through it.

This involvement matters, but isn't often happening, and isn't often effective. The CMI report that although 64% of middle managers could communicate upwards to senior leaders, many are frustrated that they are not listened to despite the opportunity (CMI, 2016) – suggesting it is not as two-way or as genuine as we might hope. Indeed, the same research shows that:
- Only 37% of middle managers believe senior leaders are transparent in their decisions and actions.
- Only 48% of middle managers believe that communication with them is prioritized by their leadership teams (CMI, 2016).

James was a middle manager at Organisation A, which was a large research and development (R&D) organisation employing around 1,000 people in the UK. They have requested anonymity for themselves and the organisation. The organisation was young, around 10 years old, and had not developed some of the internal processes around change that a more mature organisation might have. Unfortunately, whilst James was there, the organisation was buffeted by multiple large-scale changes happening simultaneously. They had a change of Chief Executive, a change in business strategy, huge financial challenges to overcome, and a pivot in terms of the sectoral focus of their R&D.

As you may be expecting, James and other middle managers were given little to no support during this period of change. Job roles and the focus of their teams changed, overnight, and James was simply expected to turn up for work and get on with things. They were left in the dark, with barely any information about what was happening or why and were told what they were expected to do.

No support was given or made available to James to plan or implement the changes. Middle managers were left alone to find out additional information about the changes, how others were affected, and how to provide support for their reports and teams during the changes.

James found that it is important for middle managers to be honest throughout change. They told their reports and teams what they knew, and what they didn't. They told their teams what they would be able to do and find out, and what they wouldn't be able to do or find out. This level of honesty kept teams engaged with the middle manager and showed that James was as affected by the changes as everyone else, bringing some authenticity to the (admittedly minimal) communications.

Following these experiences, James asked to leave their middle management position and return to an individual contributor role with no middle management responsibility. This was agreed by the organisation, but James feels that their organisation would never have considered it had they not prompted them to do so. The organisation relied heavily on formal HR processes to manage performance. James feels the only way a lack of fit (or competence) in a middle management role would have been dealt with was through a process leading to dismissal, irrespective of whether the organisation themselves had heavily contributed to the situation.

As we can see from the above example, the middle management experience is highly inconsistent across organisations. There is, therefore, still a lot to do if we are to maximise the potential for middle managers' contribution to change. But we must. They have a unique position afforded to few, appreciating both strategic priorities and operational realities. They can see both the forest and the trees (Tarakci et al, 2023) – able to connect parts of the organisational system that others cannot. In organisations where middle managers thrive, they are not just informed – they're engaged early, supported consistently, and trusted to shape how change is implemented locally. This equips them to more effectively manage resistance in their reports and teams.

Middle Managers and Handling Resistance to Change

Middle managers are important in dealing with and minimising resistance to organisational change. They have decades of experience of being human, allowing them to demonstrate empathy to better understand the fears and concerns of their reports and teams. The communication that they are at the centre of enables them to dispel uncertainty and build trust. And the involvement they can create builds engagement and enthusiasm. Let's examine these aspects.

Empathy

This is another under-utilised and under-appreciated skill. Often middle managers become middle managers due to their competence at the job underneath that position, and not necessarily because of their ability to demonstrate empathy or any of the other skills needed for effective leadership from the middle. Effective middle managers demonstrate the compassion and emotional intelligence that allow for better insight into how change messages are landing and allow for stronger relationships to be built. Doing this for individuals allows personalisation of the approach by middle managers, and helps those individuals fully grasp why change is needed.

Individuals react to change in diverse ways, and middle managers can leverage their knowledge of individuals and react and support accordingly. When a middle manager can utilise emotional intelligence and have empathy for another person, this can have a greater impact on that person than the formal authority that comes with the middle management position could have. This can be further enhanced if the middle manager displays some vulnerability and personal stories about how the change is affecting them – making the middle manager seem more human.

Coaching, which features in other chapters in this book, is a useful technique for middle managers to use in this type of situation. Coaching involves the use of incisive and powerful questions, active listening, and self-reflection. All these help to build relationships and demonstrate empathy and can help to explore blockers and change views about organisational change.

Communication

In a situation regarding organisational change there can be no such thing as over-communication, but there is such a thing as under-communication. Middle managers can directly influence the quality and quantity of communication to and from front line managers and teams. Where there are gaps in communication, it is natural for human beings to fill these gaps in their own minds by making things up. Over-communicating, on as many platforms as possible, is an effective way to combat this before it turns into passive or active resistance. Even when there is nothing to update on or say, communicating that that is the situation rather than staying silent would be recommended.

Communication, when repeated as often as possible, allows middle managers to consistently share the purpose of the change and how that contributes to the purpose of the organisation. Resistance would then not be about that, but about individual concerns. Front line managers and teams look to middle managers for clarity on why the change is happening, and regular, consistent, repeated communication provides that – it allows middle managers to promote the benefits of the change and the dangers of doing nothing.

Research from LSA Global highlights the importance of communication: top-performing managers are 13.5 times more likely to have open lines of communication, openness, and the free flow of information than their low-performing colleagues (LSA Global, 2024). Put simply, it can make the difference between effective and ineffective middle managers during change.

Involvement

Involvement of middle managers, and involvement by middle managers, would also help to take full account of the context for the change. Change will be difficult to achieve it the context is not fully considered, so involvement is key to this. Middle managers on their own may not have all the information and knowledge needed, and involvement of front line managers and teams can increase their buy-in to the change as they will feel as if they are listened to and able to influence how the change lands. Genuine and meaningful involvement, through multiple methods and covering as wide a population as is practical, will make reception by those affected more accepting, and smooth the overall change journey. Middle managers could adopt an "open door" type of approach, making themselves visible and approachable for informal discussions as well as formal feedback, both virtually and in-person. A more proactive approach may be for middle managers to have a way of initiating conversations rather than waiting for individuals to approach them.

This type of involvement may also minimise the cultural barriers and risks to effective change. Often, culture can be a blocker or cited as the reason change fails to land effectively. But involvement of those affected by it, facilitated by middle managers, can ensure that the change is not just about the what and when, but considers the organisational system in totality, translating the strategic rhetoric into practical actions that look at behaviours, decisions, ways of working. It harnesses the benefits of employee involvement to be able to express their concerns and worries, with the benefits of support from and increased visibility of middle managers in driving the change forward.

Involvement often creates greater accountability for the change from all affected by it. It can ensure that all understand their role in the change through two-way dialogue, sharing of issues and worries, and more. Workshops or individual/group coaching sessions could allow those affected by the change to work through its impact on them in a safe space, whilst influencing what happens next.

The CIPD state that change is "not a spectator sport. Everyone, from senior managers to the most junior employees, must be on the pitch participating. It is the significant cultural element of transformations that requires long-term investment beyond restructuring initiatives to generate new ways of thinking and acting" (CIPD, 2015). This reinforces how critical it is that middle managers find ways of involving, and not just informing, their reports and teams about change. All must be aligned behind the change.

Strategies to Align Teams Behind Change

Alignment matters. Middle managers must break down top-down organisational change imperatives into manageable steps, with clear milestones, so that their teams understand what to do first, and why. They must regularly update their teams on the progress of the change within the organisation and talk openly about challenges faced. They must keep their teams focused on the bigger picture by showing them how the change contributes to that, and how their own actions do likewise. Middle managers need to understand how their teams feel about the change, and this alignment process aids that.

Change, particularly when large in scale or transformational in impact, requires letting go of past ways of working and developing new ones. Many change models cover this – Bridges' Transition Model which we have explored in Chapter Three, and Lewin's Unfreeze-Change-Refreeze Model too. All of these require individuals to fully understand what the organisational vision is, why the change is necessary and what might happen if nothing was changed, and to contextualise the change to their own situation(s).

Middle managers are uniquely placed to create this alignment, since they guide their reports and teams on the activities required to effect the change required in the organisation. They can see what the change will look and feel like, whilst simultaneously understanding how performance and productivity – business as usual – is ensured. Hirsch suggests that it would be helpful for senior leaders to be mindful of this and accept short-term dips in performance whilst resources are stretched (Hirsch, 2022). This may enable middle managers to build commitment to and alignment behind the change.

Alignment requires middle managers to consider the whole organisational system, noting that change in one aspect has a consequential impact on other aspects. The middle manager can more easily see which aspects require attention, whereas front line managers and teams may only see the changes in their daily activities. If a middle manager takes a similar view, then the change could fail because of the lack of attention on other aspects of the organisational system. The creation of a shared vision by the middle manager can allow teams to align behind it because they understand the need for change better. That shared vision will bridge the gap between senior leaders' intentions and operational realities and giving clarity on direction of travel. Middle managers could facilitate the creation of this shared vision via multiple methods involving as many people as possible.

The shared vision for middle managers and their reports and teams is necessary, since the strategic imperative is quite high level and ambiguous. Left on its own, it could lead to confusion and resistance to that imperative. Shared visions from middle managers allow all affected by the change to contextualise it, build their understanding, work out precisely how they are affected by it, and what they need to do next – thereby reducing resistance.

Shared visions allow middle managers to become storytellers, and to communicate through stories, which are an important source of information and offer clarity about organisational values and the behaviours the organisation expects from its people (CIPD. 2015). Storytelling allows individuals to see themselves as part of the change, and how they might cope better with it. It allows individuals to be more engaged with the strategic narrative and imperative, acting out their roles within it and re-telling the story to others. Middle managers could lead sessions where such stories are co-created and told, using various helpful methods such as storyboards and story walls – physical representations of what the change could and should be. With training, middle managers could adopt various methods such as LEGO Serious Play to engage their reports and teams in visualising what the future situation will be.

Achieving this alignment brings together lots of different perspectives about change. Front line teams are closer to the customers of an organisation and can share customer perspectives more easily but may not see the way that their own performance may be affected by change. Their managers will see how the performance and productivity of a team may be affected by change but may not see how other parts of the organisation are similarly affected. Middle managers, though, can harness and bring together all these different and often-divergent perspectives, and it is their ability to do so that is crucial for making change work effectively. The middle manager can then feed information back up the organisation to senior leaders, having effectively aligned their teams behind the change. The main thing to do next, then, when the change takes place, is to keep morale and engagement stable, or high.

How Middle Managers Can Maintain Morale and Engagement During Change

Middle managers, once change begins, have played important roles in interpreting change, building understanding of it, and reducing blockers or resistance to it. But change can be disruptive, disturbing, and emotionally draining. A middle manager must keep morale and engagement high enough during this phase of change, by recognising and celebrating small wins, offering emotional and professional support, and advocating for their teams' concerns with senior leaders.

The good news is that middle managers are well-placed to do this, and in larger organisations are viewed as senior leaders by front line teams. They know their direct reports and teams well. They know what is likely to motivate them and will already have spent time at an earlier stage in the change interpreting it and breaking it down into actionable steps. They are also likely to be much more visible to front line teams than senior leaders could be, enabling them to sense the emotional reaction to change and to deal with those things in real time.

The leadership style adopted by the middle manager to maintain morale and engagement must be both empathetic and authentic. They must focus on relationships and not just task completion. They must be visible to front line managers and teams, both virtually and in-person, so that those managers and teams feel the middle manager is approachable and will understand their context. A middle manager who is isolated cannot do these things.

The natural leadership style should engender trust between the middle manager and their direct reports and teams. Trust can be a critical component of successful change – high-levels of trust deliver the enabling conditions in which innovation, problem-solving, knowledge-sharing and engagement will thrive (CIPD, 2015). Trust is built over time, through middle management actions as described here. If middle managers can demonstrate integrity and authenticity in the way they deal with their front-line reports and teams, trust and engagement are likely to follow. If they give their teams a voice, morale and engagement should remain a high as possible. Talking about the change and constructively challenging it allows for more tailored responses – answers – to be given and for further dialogue to take place. This is engaging in the change by beginning to explore possibilities and taps into many of the crucial aspects of models around effective change.

Tools and Frameworks for Middle Managers to use During Change

Middle managers can use a range of tools and frameworks to support their work during change. We will look at Kotter's model, the ADKAR model (picking two from many similar models), and other tools that may help them to do this.

Kotter's 8-step model (Kotter, 1996) is a familiar and often reassuring framework for middle managers to introduce and manage change with. It can harness some of the essential energies in change situations – a dissatisfaction with the current reality; an inspiring vision of the future; and some easily recognisable steps to put into action. It also focuses on how change can be embedded and sustained. The case study for this chapter shows how this has been done in practice in one organisation where I worked. It shows how Kotter's framework enables organisations to engage middle manager more in the change process and to leverage the position and knowledge middle managers must make the change more likely to succeed.

ADKAR (Hiatt, 1999) is another helpful framework for middle managers to use in change management situations. It offers a very practical set of steps that can be easily applied by middle managers:

Stage	Meaning	Practical steps for middle managers
Awareness	Ensuring employees know about the change, and why it is necessary	– Using meetings with front line teams to share the big picture / burning platform – Ensure that teams are aware of the risks inherent in the status quo remaining
Desire	Increasing the willingness of teams to support the change	– Highlight the individual and collective benefits of the change – Work to minimise resistance by listening to concerns, showing empathy, and suggesting actions that would help to reduce challenges
Knowledge	Giving the team to ability to change	– Providing training, guidance, and other means of support to enable people to acquire new knowledge and skills – Acting as a coach to reinforce application of such knowledge and skills in day-to-day work

(continued)

Stage	Meaning	Practical steps for middle managers
Ability	Putting change into practice	– Creating pilot projects for change – Giving feedback about how change is going – Identifying and going for quick wins to build some confident with, momentum behind, the change
Reinforcement	Ensuring the change sticks	– Praising and recognising those who have aligned with the change – Regularly checking-in with teams to ensure there are no new barriers

Much of the ADKAR model could, and should, be the responsibility of middle managers. Employees and teams benefit from hearing directly from middle managers about what is going on in the organisation, and this model facilitates that. Middle managers lead change by example – if they passively support or even resist a change, their direct reports are likely to do the same (Prosci, 2025) – but the ADKAR model prompts more than that.

Other useful tools and frameworks that offer benefits to middle managers include (but are not limited to):

– Serious play (involving LEGO or similar) as discussed earlier in this chapter
– Project management software that allows for multiple initiatives to be implemented and tracked, and reported on, simultaneously. These can help identify blockers to change, capacity for change, and recommended actions. It could also provide a central repository for communication, updates and more.
– Rich pictures – co-drawn representations of organisations on one piece of paper (or a virtual alternative), including sketches, cartoons, phrases, symbols and more. The visual nature encourages discussion and participation, which can increase engagement (CIPD, 2015).

All this assumes that middle managers have been given the right training and support to learn how to use these tools. Sadly, that is not usually the case. Prosci research suggested that 63% of organisations do not adequately prepare middle managers with the skills, training, and tools they need to lead through change (Prosci, 2025). Let's change that.

Case studies

In an organisation where I worked as a middle manager in the early 2010s (employing c500 staff in the UK social housing sector), we had three large scale change initiatives happening simultaneously. They were:
- A change to the terms and conditions of employment to modernise our offer to staff and reflect changed ways of working
- A move to a new-build head office whilst closing nine other locations, which because it would mean not enough space for all employees necessitated the introduction of agile and remote/hybrid working principles
- A restructure of front-line teams to optimise new service delivery models.

All three change initiatives were linked, and each had the potential to go very well, or very horribly wrong, with knock-on effects on the other two if either occurred. Middle managers like me were crucial in interpreting the changes for our front-line reports and teams, managing resistance, enabling two-way communication, and keeping engagement high whilst the changes were implemented.

Kotter's 8-step model was chosen as the overall guiding framework for coordinating all three changes – because of its sequential and easy to follow structure. We began by talking openly about the need for change to all employees, using multiple channels and methods, and taking our time to reinforce the burning platform that we had. Middle managers were tasked with talking to their own areas about what would happen if the status quo remained. We then gathered a group – a guiding coalition – of stakeholders for each of the three initiatives, plus a combined board for all three together. The sub-groups contained middle managers and representatives from the front line, and they were actively involved in determining some of the next steps. The guiding coalition board created the inspiring and clear vision of the future based on the feedback from the sub-groups, and the middle manager led sub-groups were then tasked with the creation of a communication and change management plan.

Middle managers were then empowered to work with their own areas to try out recent changes, such as changes to working patterns, use of modern technology, new ways of rewarding employees – all called pilot schemes. They were tasked with capturing lessons learnt from these pilots, and in sharing quick wins and early successes openly across the organisation. We spent time ensuring those experimenting with change – regardless of whether it worked or not – were recognised for their efforts. They also shared challenges and barriers to the success of the changes, which enabled the final stages to be assembled.

The middle manager led sub-groups were then asked to create ways to ensure the changes happened on time, and as smoothly as possible, and created their own sets of recommendations for doing so. Using links to organisational values, visible praise for those embracing the change, and additional support and training for people, the middle managers were given freedom to ensure that the changes were sustained within the organisation.

Case study reflections

In the case study in this chapter, the following points stand out for further reflection:
- Sometimes grouping change initiatives together to consider them as one programme can be helpful in co-ordinating action from middle managers
- The Kotter model is straightforward, and gives a step-by-step framework to consider and follow
- Spending time warming employees up to the change is an effective use of middle management time
- Including middle managers and their reports and teams in the broader guiding coalition can build engagement with the change
- Likewise, involving them in designing the communication of the change can generate more engagement and buy-in
- Giving middle managers the empowerment to try new things, give recognition for what has worked and for what didn't work, can be effective ways of keeping morale and momentum high
- Ensuring that middle managers could recommend how to further embed the change can give them some responsibility and accountability for making it work

Action Plan

If you wish to enable middle managers to more effectively lead change from the middle, reflecting on the following questions is likely to help:
- There are many change roles that a middle manager could play. Which do you intend they play, and how will you equip them to do so effectively?
- How will you provide time and space for middle managers to make sense of change to themselves as individual employees?
- What kind of peer support / community of practice for middle managers will you create to ensure that they can talk to each other about change?
- How will your senior leaders engage meaningfully with middle managers about change, and involve them in shaping the change?

- What is the level of empathy skills amongst your middle managers, and how can you build more?
- How will you over-communicate during change?
- How will you encourage middle managers to have an "open door" both virtually and in-person?
- What will your middle managers do to actively involve and engage their teams about change?
- What support do middle managers need to break strategic imperatives about change into practical steps?
- Who needs to know about a short-term dip in performance whilst teams wrestle with change, and how will they be informed?
- How will you support middle managers in creating shared visions for change with their teams?
- What use will you make of storytelling, rich picturing, and serious play, as tools for middle managers to utilise during change?
- How can you increase the empathetic, authentic leadership style needed by middle managers?
- How will you equip your middle managers to make use of frameworks such as Kotter's 8-step model, ADKAR, and project management software, to facilitate change?

References

CIPD (2015) *Landing transformational change – closing the gap between theory* . . . Available at: https://www.cipd.org/globalassets/media/knowledge/knowledge-hub/reports/landing-transformation-change_2015-gap-theory-practice_tcm18-9050.pdf

CMI (2016) *The Middle Manager Lifeline.* Available at: https://www.managers.org.uk/knowledge-and-insights/research/the-middle-manager-lifeline/

Hirsch, W. (2023) *Three ways middle managers succeed at organizational change.* Available at: https://wendyhirsch.com/blog/middle-manager-change-success-steps

Kempton, L. (2025) *CLARC: The role of People Managers in change management.* Available at: https://www.prosci.com/blog/clarc-the-role-of-people-managers-in-change-management

Kotter, J. (1999) *Leading change.* Harvard Business School.

LSA Global (2024) *Organizational Alignment Research Model.* Available at: https://lsaglobal.com/insights/proprietary-methodology/lsa-3x-organizational-alignment-model/

Prosci (2025) *The PROSCI ADKAR® model.* Available at: https://www.prosci.com/methodology/adkar

Tarakci, M., Heyden, M.L.M., Rouleau, L., Raes, A. and Floyd, S.W. (2023), Heroes or Villains? Recasting Middle Management Roles, Processes, and Behaviours. J. Manage. Stud., 60: 1663–1683. https://doi.org/10.1111/joms.12989

Winston, A., Polman, P. and Seabright, J. (2023) *Middle Management is the key to sustainability.* Available at: https://hbr.org/2023/11/middle-management-is-the-key-to-sustainability

Chapter Five
Emotional Intelligence In Middle Management

Throughout earlier chapters we have examined how much of success as a middle manager comes from understanding and getting the best from people. We have hinted strongly at the role played by Emotional Intelligence (EI) and will explore this in more depth in this chapter. We will look at why EI matters in middle management, and how middle managers can develop the self-awareness needed to be emotionally intelligent. We will look at how middle managers can use EI to enhance individual and team performance, build trust, resolve conflicts, and make communication more effective.

The Importance of Ei

Many theorists have examined what EI is and its role in facilitating better communication within teams – how it can build stronger ties and relationships between people, and how it can improve decision-making and organisational outcomes. But why does it matter so much in middle management?

Meg Gorman is a manager who has occupied many senior and middle management positions across her career, mostly working within exceptionally large global financial organisations. Gorman is based in the UK, and we talked about her experiences of middle managers who displayed a lot or little of emotional intelligence.

Gorman spoke first about a manager she had worked for who displayed a lot of emotional intelligence. This manager had a varied background and what Gorman described as a non-traditional route into middle management. However, this varied experience of doing lots of distinct roles seemed to instil in them high levels of emotional intelligence – they could read people and situations very well and always seemed to know what to say and do (and when to say or do little). They could build trust through strong relationships and actively encouraged other middle managers to do so. They were able to exert a strong influence on organisational culture and were a calming presence at times of crisis. They never lost sight of what their front-line reports and teams did but also displayed leadership skills that were a requirement of senior roles. This person changed Gorman's view of what leadership and middle management were. She saw how this person could achieve more by speaking less and used silence as well as incisive questioning to prompt others into action and therefore be seen to be even more influential. Gorman consciously strove to mirror this behaviour – she had previously thought that a middle manager needed to be the most vocal person in the room.

Gorman then told me about a middle manager she had worked for who had little, perhaps no, emotional intelligence. She cited a time when she had suffered a bereavement of a close relative and was struggling at work for obvious reasons. Gorman was accessing support outside of work but could not access this inside work, leaving her with 40+ hours of the week where she felt isolated and in trouble. She needed more support in work to enable her to remain there and be productive. Gor-

https://doi.org/10.1515/9783111713526-005

man's manager refused to acknowledge Gorman's regular panic attacks and branded her unpredictable and volatile behaviour as misbehaviour instead. Gorman provided medical evidence to support her claim for more support, but her manager threatened to take away Gorman's management responsibility unless Gorman improved her attitude and behaviour. Gorman was forced to complain about this manager, but the experience changed her and made her wary of engaging with people and showing vulnerability, of being her authentic self at work.

In the example above, we see how a middle manager displaying high levels of EI resulted in positive outcomes, and how a middle manager with low or no levels of EI resulted in the opposite. In my career I have experienced similar too. When I went through a painful and public divorce, my manager at the time showed empathy, understanding, support, and a concern for me as a human being rather than a concern for how my stresses could impact the organisation. I rebounded quicker from that situation than I might have done otherwise, and with increased loyalty to both that middle manager and the organisation. Conversely, several years later when my wife was having a difficult pregnancy and my mum was in the initial stages of a terminal illness, I needed more flexibility in my working arrangements and looked to my then-manager for support but got none. I was told to "man up," that everyone had issues, and the expectation was that we all got on with them outside work and didn't let them affect us IN work. My commitment dropped, my performance and health suffered, and I left that organisation – or rather, that manager – just a couple of weeks later.

It is no surprise that research suggests that relationships with management are the top factor in employees job satisfaction, but also the second most important determinant of their overall wellbeing (Allas and Schaninger, 2020). And yet, as we have examined in earlier chapters, few middle managers reach that position based on the strength of their ability to create job satisfaction or positively impact wellbeing. Indeed, they are often promoted because they can be self-centred, overconfident, narcissistic, arrogant, manipulative, and risk-prone (Allas and Schaninger, 2020). This makes it more important that we identify the right skillsets and mindsets well before an employee achieves middle management status, and/or that we develop those skills and mindsets as soon as possible once that level is achieved. Only then can middle managers create the psychologically safe environment and culture that delivers trust, engagement, and strong relationships.

Wendy Hubbard has been a middle manager in the UK's National Health Service (NHS) since 2009, and spoke to me about her experiences working in a hospital, and how they contrasted with previous experiences working for a large hospitality chain and running her own pub. Hubbard, like so many in this book, had received no management training before becoming a manager, learning entirely on the job.

When Hubbard joined the NHS, she had been a manager in the hospitality industry for many years, but the difference in context and culture was stark. Hubbard was running her own pub, being the sole arbiter in decision-making and problem-solving and operating very flexibly. In the NHS, she encountered a very hierarchical structure, with a command-and-control type of management in her area, with little embracing of change or innovative ideas.

Hubbard' own manager saw her as a threat. Hubbard had been creating standardised documentation for the ten team leaders who reported to her – this was because they too had had no training as managers, and she wanted to create some consistency between them as well as give them some support. Her own manager rejected Hubbard' initiative out of hand because it was new and not authorised from above. Hubbard felt this manager was dismissive, rude, and would talk down to her in front of others. Hubbard described how the manager had The Glare (capitalised deliberately, since Hubbard and her colleagues all knew about its power) and would tap her nails on a desk without speaking to gain silence and attention. Unsurprisingly this manager used to make Hubbard frustrated and sometimes see her heading home to cry – whilst Hubbard wanted to improve how things were done, she felt her manager just wanted to "squash" her.

When the wider department was going through major organisational changes, Hubbard would try to make her direct reports and teams feel better about the changes and come to terms with them more, trying to engage them. Her manager would actively un-do what Hubbard was doing, and to her it felt like the manager didn't want improvements that they hadn't personally suggested. Hubbard describes this manager as "being on a power trip," having no social skills and no emotional intelligence, despite lots of business-relevant skills. In time, when faced with a decision or problem, Hubbard began asking herself "what would my manager do?" and then consciously do the opposite.

Sadly, Hubbard' experience prior to this in the hospitality business had some similarities despite the different level of empowerment and autonomy, showing that empowerment and autonomy alone cannot liberate middle managers. In the hospitality business Hubbard, with an exceptionally good attendance record, suffered an injury in a road traffic accident. She continued to work until the pain became too much, and she was taken to the Accident & Emergencies ward. Hubbard was away from work for two days and kept her manager informed. She was later reprimanded by a senior manager for being in the Accident & Emergencies ward instead of at work, with the manager citing all the work that had not been done during this time. The manager also said that being in hospital was no excuse for not doing what a manager should be doing in terms of managing the team. Again, there was a lack of emotional intelligence here, and this experience alone was enough to prompt Hubbard to seek a demotion from her middle management position and later leave the hospitality business.

The example above is another that illustrates the power of EI within middle management, and the impact it can have. Examining EI and its impact allows us to see differences in leadership styles. A transactional leadership style, focused on achieving levels of performance, and controlling both sanctions and rewards for achieving/not achieving those levels, would naturally respect and aim for compliance with processes and rules, and in protecting structure and authority. Conversely, a more transformational leadership style, focused on motivating individuals and teams to want to perform, would focus on emotions and values, and in guiding through inspiration and enthusiasm. The transformational style is therefore one that consciously adopts EI principles. Emotionally intelligent leaders are transformational leaders who are great at interpersonal relationships, fostering collaboration and inspiring trust. And EI can separate the great middle managers from the ordinary or poor ones:

- Employees who report to high EI middle managers perform better on the job and report higher job satisfaction
- Employees with high EI middle managers engage more in organisational citizenship behaviours such as altruism, being sporting, conscientiousness, and civic virtue
- Middle managers with high EI have higher employee retention (Sass, 2025)

Sara spoke to me about her background as a middle manager in large multinational corporations. She observes that most middle managers that she worked alongside didn't have the right people management capabilities to do what their teams needed, nor the time to do so effectively.

Sara feels there is often confusion about what middle management should be doing. She cited one of her own experiences where all her stakeholders would repeatedly tell her she was a great manager and had formal performance conversations where she was told that everyone loved her but that she was not a top performer. This was because her comparative performance statistics were not placing her as a top performer – and yet everyone said she was brilliant. She felt confused about what brilliant might have meant, and concluded that people management skills were not valued as highly as operational delivery was.

She feels that middle managers should be human-centred. She had a new start direct report who had a lot of personal issues but was hesitant to ask her for support, or to ask to move meetings by sometimes only 15 minutes to help with childcare issues. Sara feels that if more middle managers could be human-centred and look at what is affecting people, it would help everyone. She feels that a reason for this is that organisations don't pay that enough attention – if a middle manager is not human-centred, then the risks are considered minimal by organisations.

And yet, if they do fail, the consequences can be disastrous. In one role, Sara and her team moved into another team that was under scrutiny and about which there was discussion about whether the team had a future with the organisation. The manager responsible for the team's work would not give them any clarity about their roles for six months, leaving the team alone and in the dark and not communicating with them. When Sara would prompt them to give them some clarity, the manager would say they didn't have time. Engagement levels plummeted, and anxiety levels role. Bizarrely, the clarity could have been given – the team DID have a future, and all jobs WERE safe, but because the manager didn't share what was known or quell natural worries, many people left the team and organisation before finding out the truth.

Sara ensured that she was human-centred by taking a coaching qualification and consciously developing coaching skills in her team too. That helped her listen more to their issues and focus on helping them resolve them. It helped her to get people to come to terms with their role easier, the context in which they operated, and to manage their emotions better.

As the example above and elsewhere in this chapter show, the better middle managers show empathy for others' situations. They show compassion and are not afraid to confront and deal with emotions. This helps them to be more authentic, to build employee confidence in their actions and behaviours. The better middle managers can easily judge a situation and are aware of how their behaviours may be judged in turn. And employees need this – in our technologically advanced (and advancing) age, artificial intelligence and other technologies can easily perform some (perhaps many) of the tasks middle managers usually undertake. But technology cannot replace the human elements that we have been discussing here – empathy, transformational leadership, compassion, and more. We need human middle managers who understand their own attributes, who can respond to adversity with resilience and maintain their composure, and who can manage stress and conflict with empathy and effective communication. These all result in employees feeling valued. However, research has found that 68% of organisations have no way of recognising or enhancing emotional intelligence amongst their employees (Greevy, 2025), let alone their middle managers – there is appreciation therefore that EI matters, but scarce resources provided for its development. If we do not ensure that our middle managers possess good to great EI, and possess instead strong technical skills and knowledge, they could be ineffective within the organisation. The good news is that EI is a skillset and mindset that can be developed over time through habit formation, repetition, and reflection. Middle managers should be given support to build the following aspects (presented in no order of priority):

- Listening well – not assuming that they do, or should, know more or better than their direct reports and teams
- Focusing their attention and efforts on what they can control, and expecting positive outcomes from that
- Noticing and naming their own emotions, and doing the same for others
- Communicating honestly and openly
- Assertiveness – setting boundaries in tricky situations and with difficult people
- Being inquisitive – asking questions to find out more about situations and people
- Finding light in dark situations through use of appropriate humour
- Consistently and openly recognising achievements and successes
- Focusing on relationships not just with their direct reports and teams, but across the organisation – remembering that sometimes it isn't about what you know, but who you know
- Showing vulnerability, allowing feedback to be responded to appropriately rather than having an impervious thick skin

- Reflecting on situations and learning from mistakes
- Prioritising values as much as results – focusing on the way they and other people behave, rather than obsessing about their outputs
- Providing autonomy to their front-line reports and teams to make decisions without fear of micromanagement

But to do this, we need to begin by developing middle managers sense of self-awareness and self-insight. Let's look at why and how to do this.

Developing Middle Manager Self-Awareness

Self-awareness is an especially important aspect for middle managers to develop. Through seeking regular feedback from those they interact with directly and indirectly, reflecting on their own style and its impact, and identifying their own personal triggers and biases, they can become more rounded as leaders and become more human-centred in their approach. A middle manager who is self-aware can more easily manage themselves before doing the same for others.

Self-awareness includes recognising one's own emotional state and that of others, and the impact that each can have on the other. In middle management, with its unique position, this becomes even more important – we have noted how relationships matter more in middle management and knowing the impact one has on others is crucial in building and maintaining effective relationships. It has been found to be crucial for job performance – 83% of people high in self-awareness are top performers, with just 2% being bottom performers (Brown and Nwagbara, 2021). However, whilst 95% of people believe they are self-aware, research suggests that only 10–15% are (Harvard Business School, 2019). This lack of self-awareness could cause many problems in middle management given the potentially very wide impact that they have. Just as self-aware middle managers can positively impact the behaviour of others, middle managers lacking self-awareness could negatively – and destructively – impact that behaviour.

There are several effective methods to develop self-awareness in middle managers. These include:

- 360-degree feedback. Regardless of whether done manually or using technology, this method would allow a middle manager to compare their own performance and views on behaviour and its impact with the opinions of others. It would allow the middle manager to examine how they are perceived by others and uncover any potential blind spots. Including feedback from people the middle manager is close to outside of work – friends, family – would let the middle manager see whether there are aspects of their personality that are more easily seen outside of work which could be helpful inside work.

–   Journalling or other reflective log activity. A regular record and reflection of what has happened to the middle manager and their emotional reaction to what has happened may help that middle manager to make sense of situations, and to realise what aspects of their behaviour led to either positive or negative outcomes.

–   Taking time after each interaction. A few minutes after each interaction to reflect on how that went, noticing and labelling each emotion, might enable the middle manager to identify what prompted the emotional response, and to process it accordingly. With practice this can become near instantaneous and in the moment reflection.

–   Practicing active observation. Middle managers interact with a very wide range of stakeholders and can achieve much by noticing what is going on, paying attention to the interactions of others, as well as their body language and non-verbal cues. If this becomes a habit, combined with some of the other aspects noted above, it can aid the middle manager in beginning to anticipate the outcome of a situation before it develops, and to take appropriate action to influence that.

–   Noticing links between non-work-related parts of the middle managers life, and work. For example, quality of diet and nutrition, hydration, relationships outside work, quality of sleep, and more. This could help the middle manager to develop healthy habits outside of work to better influence their behaviour inside work.

–   Self-assessment. There are many available competency or leadership behaviour frameworks for middle managers to use. Self-assessing against any of these may enable middle managers to identify things that they are weaker at – and become consciously incompetent rather than unconsciously incompetent at those things. For example, a middle manager may be strong at verbal communication but weak on written communication and seeing this presented in a self-assessment may lead to more informed choices about communication methods being made. It might also lead to greater and more informed reflection on past situations where either strengths or weaknesses have been in play for the middle manager.

There could be many ways to create confidence and competence in using these different methods to build self-awareness. Workshops and formal courses obviously have their place but take middle managers away from their work. It may be more convenient to build habits for middle managers that include micro learning methods that teach and embed skills in the moment, and which build skill practice into their working days. Creating (and facilitating) a dynamic community of practice where peer coaching can take place is also helpful since it could encourage middle managers to raise issues when they occur and access help almost immediately. An on-demand coach or mentor, accessible via text or live chatting, could aid instantaneous reflection and provide a useful mirror for the middle manager.

An extremely helpful model to help middle managers (and indeed anyone) achieve greater levels of self-awareness is the Ladder of Inference, created by Chris Argyris in 1970. This model illustrates how we metaphorically climb a mental ladder of our assumptions and beliefs based on how we interpret and filter our experiences, affected by our biases and history (Dickerson, 2024). We all look at data and information differently and use some and discard other data as we ascend the Ladder. Further up, we interpret data and assign meaning to it, making assumptions, and filling in gaps, before reaching a conclusion that seems both obvious, and impermeable to other evidence.

Knowing about the Ladder and how it shapes our view of the world is a conscious development that moves the middle manager from a state of unconscious incompetence and towards consciousness. Dickerson likens this to breathing – paid no attention, it happens automatically, but when one notices breathing, it can be controlled – become intentional (Dickerson, 2024). Knowing about the Ladder means that middle managers can become more aware of their behaviours and actions and, therefore, more intentional about them. I have used this in coaching sessions for middle managers to enable them to reflect more deeply on their thought processes and assumptions to work out why they behaved or acted the way they did. It has enabled middle managers I have coached to explore what other choices could have been made and where that might have led, and to consider how to leverage new options in the future.

Greater self-awareness is also useful in resolving conflict and improving communication, and we will now look at how these can be done more effectively by middle managers.

Resolving conflict and EI

Middle managers can use emotional intelligence to help them resolve conflicts. EI helps the middle manager to have open discussions to surface underlying issues, to mediate effectively whilst keeping a focus on shared goals, and to establish clear guidelines for respectful communication amongst their reports and teams. But how do they do this?

Many organisational conflicts are caused by misunderstandings and a general lack of EI. Emotions play a strong role in conflict, and this can be exacerbated when people can't recognise or understand them, or when they can't process or express them. Middle managers are likely to see and experience more conflict given their wide stakeholder base and the range of interactions they will have, so they need the confidence and competence to be able to address conflict early, and/or effectively. The types of self-awareness building activities covered in this chapter could give insight into the middle managers' style and normal ways of handling conflict. They could also help the middle manager to be more aware of others' body language, tone, and emotional state, helping them to know individuals and teams better.

Stronger relationships are at the heart of both EI and effective conflict handling. If the middle manager knows individuals well, they could anticipate sources of conflict before they occur, as well as factor in any outside work influences that may have a bearing on how individuals relate to each other. A middle manager with strong relationships will know each of their direct reports preferred working styles, and their ways of expressing frustration or dealing with stress. Often when coaching managers, I ask them whether they know the answers to some questions about those they work most closely with:

- What is the name of their partner (if they have one)?
- What are the names of their children or pets (if they have them)?
- What is the one biggest thing worrying them outside of work?
- Who is their closest friend at work?
- What is the one biggest thing worrying them inside of work?

It always surprises me how many middle managers don't have answers to all those questions. I then encourage them to find out the answers, but not in a direct, questioning way – find naturally occurring opportunities to do it. But knowing the answers to these questions enables a middle manager not just to anticipate potential conflict, but to plan for how to best deal with it.

The middle managers' emotional intelligence should enable them to have a good sense of the strength (or lack of) of relationships between their direct reports and teams. An EI-strong middle manager will have put in place regular meetings with all stakeholders and will be comfortable discussing frustrations and concerns with them. Their awareness of body language and tone would enable them to pick up not just on things that are said and done, but things that are not said and done, enabling them to step in early and have informal discussions if they sense a conflict about to erupt. Doing this early displays some of the right behaviour and values that middle managers should develop – that conflict can be serious, and the middle manager will not let it go unchallenged or unresolved. It also helps reinforce the sense that the culture is a psychologically safe one where individuals are treated as adults by the middle manager who promotes openness, respect, and consistency. Sometimes, those involved may not realise their contribution to the emerging conflict so an early intervention could prevent things escalating.

An emotionally intelligent middle manager will know whether someone else's style, background and way of working is likely to mesh well with others or be a potential cause of conflict and will address that with them privately to raise awareness of potential issues. They will also be keenly aware of the impact that their own style and behaviour as a middle manager has on others, that they are role modelling the values and behaviours that others will see as important – and choose the right positive aspects for others to see because of that.

When conflict does occur, the emotionally intelligent middle manager is well equipped to deal with it because of their level of self-awareness, relationship management, and more. Things that will help include:

– Asking questions to fully understand what is happening, what has caused it, and the different perspectives and needs in the situation
– Using the Ladder of Inference to explore assumptions and interpretations in the conflict, as well as how things could play out differently if other filters were applied (or if none were)
– Showing empathy, and encouraging others to do the same, for different perspectives so that the conflict can be seen from all angles
– Encouraging contributions from all sides to jointly solve problems and brainstorm solutions, and respecting contributions when they are shared

An emotionally intelligent middle manager will also be able to effectively spot whether, following the initial intervention, the conflict has been adequately resolved, or whether there are lingering feelings of resentment. This can be done through individual meetings as well as the regular observation and listening that an EI-strong middle manager will be doing. But much more can be achieved – and potentially avoided – if the middle manager leverages the communication skills and methods, they have access to.

Communication and EI

We have examined how important effective communication is earlier chapters. Here we will show how it correlates with elevated levels of emotional intelligence, where a middle manager can ensure clarity of expectations and goals, foster open dialogue and ensure their reports and teams have input to generate buy-in, and build stronger rapport and trust.

Nick Holmes is the Vice President for Learning and Culture at Avalere Health, a healthcare innovations organisation with a global reach. Holmes spoke with me about his time as a middle manager and his role in developing middle managers.

Holmes spoke about his background in acting and performing, and how that prepared him unknowingly for middle management. In performing, Holmes had to practice relatability, building rapport with lots of new people, and focusing on his interpersonal skills to more effectively convey those in his acting. It helped him to build and adapt his own EI, and to learn the importance of both empathy and vulnerability. Crucial was the practicing of improvising, which helped him to know when to say things and when not to, what to say and what to avoid. As a middle manager and drawing on these experiences and skills, he focused on finding affinity with people to build better relationships, and in being both likeable and convincing others that they were too. Holmes says that whilst these are great skills for an actor to have, they are also great skills for a middle manager to have, and can be taught through observation, listening, and practice.

In a recent restructure, Holmes's team was halved in size and, whilst this can often be a horrific experience for those affected, Holmes found that most thanked him for how he had behaved. This was because he demonstrated genuine empathy, spent a lot of time with individuals, and respected the emotions that they were experiencing. He feels it is important for middle managers to stay connected to the front lines, avoiding cultural disconnect and deterioration. Holmes made the point that in some environments, particularly larger organisations, middle management can be indistinguishable from senior leaders, and particularly where functions such as HR are distant, indistinguishable from HR too.

In the above example we see how empathy, EI and effective communication skills make a difference in middle management roles. Communication matters in organisations but is often not highly effective. Research suggests that 86% of employees cite ineffective communication as a reason for workplace failures, that 44% of employees report a lack of effective communication as the leading cause of stress in the workplace, but that organisations with effective communication are 20% more likely to achieve above average performance (Imutan, 2024). With middle managers needing to co-ordinate important but complex information passing both up and down (and often across) the organisation, they need to be strong communicators and leverage their emotional intelligence to make communication effective. Research by the CMI showed that middle managers who can actively seek staff opinions, hold discussions, maintain open-door policies, and demonstrate approachability and interest in employee wellbeing are more effective (CMI, 2016). Some communication methods that an EI-strong middle manager could and should leverage include:

–   Using technology to connect people in real-time if they are dispersed, and providing access to written information to answer questions that an employee may have if working asynchronously. Both communication software and project management tools would be helpful here.

- Regularly meeting not just with their direct reports, but front-line teams too – ensuring that all are kept informed and up to date about recent events and happenings and can raise concerns and contribute suggestions.
- Using the open-door approach, whether virtually or in-person, so that employees know that the middle manager is accessible to them and will listen carefully to any concerns they have and seek to better understand their individual perspective and needs.
- Facilitating team development activities where shared goals, how to coordinate activities across teams, and strengthening relationships are all discussed. This could involve team development work across different teams so that the interfaces between them are explored and strengthened.

The emotionally intelligent middle manager can achieve much. The latter points hint at their role in team development – across multiple teams – and this, and their role as coach and mentor to those teams, is something we will explore in our next chapter.

Case Studies

Nancy Parks is the HR Director at Informa Festivals, a B2B events-focused business with around 1,000 colleagues that is part of Informa. Prior to that Parks had been Chief People Office at Ascential, which was later acquired by Informa. She has been both a middle manager, and responsible for developing middle managers, for many years across her career.

Parks describes middle managers as "the Magnificent Middle," a phrase I wish I had used for the title of this book! In Ascential, she put in place an approach where the organisation clarified what they wanted from their middle managers before anyone became one. This was in response to problems encountered with a lack of preparation of and awareness by prospective middle managers.

Parks had noticed that a lot of issues faced by middle managers were because of poor communication, or misaligned goals and expectations. She believed that these were unintentional consequences, but often serious and with significant impact on performance and employee relations. This was particularly noticeable in a lack of resilience when middle managers were faced with rapid, large scale organisational change. A common theme connecting all these middle management issues was a highly inconsistent level of emotional intelligence amongst that group.

With Parks seeing emotional intelligence as key to being an effective middle manager, Ascential asked all existing and potential middle managers to be clear on who they were, focusing on developing their self-awareness and understanding of their own styles and preferences. Personality and psychometric profiling tools, with associated individual coaching, were deployed to help build self-awareness. Parks was conscious that for many, growing self-awareness would lead to a realisation that they did not possess the qualities that Ascential needed in its middle managers. This was deliberate – Parks intended the middle managers to become consciously, instead of unconsciously, incompetent, before building their competence.

Parks and her team developed three pillars to help middle managers prepare for and learn about their roles – Self; Individuals; and Teams. Each pillar contained a range of learning methods – online self-study resources supported by facilitated face-to-face sessions. Each of the pillars saw a Charter developed that set out the expectations and requirements of middle managers in that pillar. For example, the Individuals Charter contained statements about empathy and trust, about celebrating difference and recognising individual achievements, and about personalising management. The Teams Charter included statements on communication, and team dynamics, and on conflict management and problem-solving. The development methods employed helped to build middle managers' competence and competence to live up to and bring each Charter to life.

Ascential also created a Community of Practice for middle managers hosted on Slack. This was led by middle management champions, identified from within their own ranks. They would lead on the sharing of knowledge and good practice, the sharing of mistakes and the learning from those, and encourage other middle managers to contribute to the Community. Amongst the aims of that Community was that it would encourage middle managers to develop and display empathy, greater self-awareness, support of others, communication skills, and more aspects related to emotional intelligence.

Parks reports that the development programme has seen around seventy-five middle managers, from a population of around two hundred, go through so far. Feedback to date has been incredibly positive.

Case Study Reflections

In the Ascential case study, the following points stand out for further reflection:
- Defining what a middle manager is, and the expectations of being one, is a good step in positioning it as a viable and attractive career option.

- Middle managers who have arrived in that role via a range of career paths are likely to have highly inconsistent levels of emotional intelligence, and taking stock of this is a good start point.
- Using self-awareness building methods, it is important to intentionally move middle managers from unconscious incompetence to conscious incompetence.
- A Charter of commitments and expectations, divided up by area of focus, and supported by development routes, is a useful way to clarify and make explicit what a middle manager does.
- A facilitated Community of Practice is helpful in encouraging middle managers to display vulnerability and support each other.

Action Plan

If you are wanting to get middle managers to become more emotionally intelligent and leverage the benefits that this can bring, answering the following questions will help:

- How clear are you on the right skillset and mindset that a middle manager needs to succeed in the role?
- What will you do to develop and encourage transformational leadership styles within the organisation?
- What methods will you deploy to develop emotional intelligence in middle managers?
- How will you support middle managers in developing their self-awareness?
- How could the Ladder of Inference help you to coach middle managers (and encourage them to do the same for others)?
- How many of your middle managers know their direct reports well enough to answer the questions posed about them?
- How will you help middle managers to reflect on their approach to resolving conflict?
- What communication methods do middle managers need to utilise more of in the organisation, and how will they be supported to do so?

References

Allas, T. and Schaninger, B. (2020) *The boss factor: Making the world a better place through workplace relationships, McKinsey & Company*. Available at: https://www.mckinsey.com/capabilities/people-

and-organizational-performance/our-insights/the-boss-factor-making-the-world-a-better-place-through-workplace-relationships#/

Brown, C. & Nwagbara, U. (2021). Leading Change with the Heart: Exploring the Relationship between Emotional Intelligence and Transformational Leadership in the Era of Covid-19 Pandemic Challenges. Economic Insights – Trends and Challenges. 2021. 1–12. 10.51865/EITC.2021.03.01. Available at: https://www.researchgate.net/publication/354497715_Leading_Change_with_the_Heart_Exploring_the_Relationship_between_Emotional_Intelligence_and_Transformational_Leadership_in_the_Era_of_Covid-19_Pandemic_Challenges

CMI (2016) *The Middle Manager Lifeline*. Available at: fhttps://www.managers.org.uk/knowledge-and-insights/research/the-middle-manager-lifeline/

Dickerson, C. (2024) *Building self-awareness to be a better human-centered leader, Harvard Business Publishing*. Available at: https://www.harvardbusiness.org/the-ladder-of-inference-building-self-awareness-to-be-a-better-human-centered-leader/

Greevy, E.M. (2025) *The importance of emotional intelligence in the workplace*. Available at: https://emperform.co.uk/blog/the-importance-of-emotional-intelligence-in-the-workplace/

Harvard Business School (2019) *Emotional intelligence in leadership: Why it's important*. Available at: https://online.hbs.edu/blog/post/emotional-intelligence-in-leadership

Imutan, J. (2024) *Bridging the gap: Building and maintaining stakeholder relationships in middle management*. Available at: https://jordanimutan.medium.com/bridging-the-gap-building-and-maintaining-stakeholder-relationships-in-middle-management-d6c176feda24

Sass, M. (2025) *Emotional intelligence and leadership: What's the connection?, TalentSmartEQ*. Available at: https://www.talentsmarteq.com/emotional-intelligence-and-leadership-whats-the-connection/

Chapter Six
The People Factor

The role of middle managers in developing others is often underappreciated and an underutilised aspect of their skillset. In this chapter we will examine how middle managers can coach and mentor their direct reports and teams. We will begin by exploring how middle managers can use coaching and mentoring skillsets and mindsets to develop others, and how they can balance doing this with their other responsibilities. We will then look at how team development in a more general sense can be facilitated by middle managers, using different methods and different tools and models.

Why are Coaching and Mentoring Essential Skills For Middle Managers?

Coaching

Coaching is often cited as a desirable skill for managers in general, and rightly so. I would go further as I believe it is an essential skill for middle managers, helping them to support the development of others by enhancing their performance. It can also help middle managers to address skills gaps to prepare for the future, and boost team morale and engagement by being visibly invested in their growth.

There is a need for middle managers to be effective at coaching. Good management increasingly requires strong collaboration and communication skills, and we have noted that middle managers need to be able to collaborate and communicate with a very wide range of stakeholders. Coaching their direct reports and teams to be more effective is an effective way of empowering them to work better together, and therefore with that wider group of stakeholders. But it is often helpful when middle managers ask questions instead of giving orders, if they support and guide instead of chiding, and where they foster growth instead of telling people what to do. The ability to coach is something that, now, could mark a middle manager as being different to other managers and potentially distinct from artificial intelligence (AI) efficiency tools because of the human aspect of coaching. Many AI tools can act as coaches but can't demonstrate the empathy and social skills that a human being can. Middle managers can't necessarily compete with AI tools on knowledge grounds – they can't be expected to have all the answers to technical queries, but they could compete on social skills if given the opportunity. And increasingly it is social skills that will make the difference in

https://doi.org/10.1515/9783111713526-006

organisations and in organisational relationships, as we have already noted in earlier chapters. However, this could lead to conflict for some middle managers, who would have to reconcile the need to coach with the remaining responsibilities they have to co-ordinate work and performance – something we will return to shortly.

Organisations adopting a command-and-control type of management are becoming less competitive and less prevalent. In their place is a management model where managers give support and guidance, instil adaptability and flexibility in their teams, building innovation and commitment. These are things that coaches do (Ibarra and Scoular, 2019). Sadly, 24% of middle managers overestimate their ability to coach (Ibarra and Scoular, 2019) despite only 30–40% of managers having been trained how to do it (MindTools, 2024).

Middle managers must first have a clear understanding of why they should coach. The need to understand how, when and where it could take place – whether that is through formal coaching, or informal conversations – and likely both. They may need to understand not just when coaching could help, but when not to use it. They need to know what the skills are that a coaching middle manager needs to use, and how to develop them if they don't already have them (and some will). There is a lot to do to raise the levels of coaching, but significant benefits if it can be done. It is also an effective use of the experience and expertise that middle managers ought to have – they can support newer, less experienced managers and show that the organisation promotes development and growth. Other benefits of coaching done well by middle managers include:

- Improving employee perception of job performance, service quality, and citizenship behaviour
- Greater role clarity, job satisfaction, and organisational commitment from employees (Ahrens et al, 2018)

But coaching is not the only tool that middle managers could deploy here to develop their teams. Mentoring is also useful.

Mentoring

Mentoring is another under-appreciated skill for middle managers. 76% of employees in one study felt that mentorship was important, but only 37% of them had a mentor (Reeves, 2023). Mentorship is felt to be important because it utilises the skills and experience of middle managers and highlights that growth and development is prioritised by the organisation – and are actively connecting employees to opportunities for that growth and development.

Mentoring can encourage cross-departmental collaboration, which is a key aspect of middle management. It can help to reduce silo-thinking and improve organisational learning and knowledge management, through careful matching of mentors and mentees. If the matching process results in middle managers mentoring someone outside of their direct reporting structure, then it could encourage other employees to communicate with and share knowledge and advice with others outside of their teams too, as well as enhancing the visibility and reputation of middle managers. It could lead to more effective communication across the organisation due to improved and stronger relationships between teams.

Almost 70% of organisations report increases in productivity due to mentoring, and improvements in employee engagement also (Reeves, 2023). But for middle managers, there are additional benefits:

- Middle managers can be more satisfied with their own jobs and more committed to their organisations than those who are not mentors
- Middle managers judged as effective mentors by their direct reports tend to have higher performance ratings from senior leaders
- New middle managers can transition better into the role if they have previously been mentored by more experienced middle managers
- Middle managers who mentor are perceived by others as more effective leaders, a greater sense of wellbeing, and stronger personal and professional networks
- Middle managers who mentor have quicker access to job-related and organisational news (Gentry and Walsh, 2025)

All this sounds like good news. But how do middle managers find the time to do this in and around their other responsibilities? How do they not just allocate the time, but set the boundaries between when they are coaching, mentoring, or enacting other middle management responsibilities?

Balancing Coaching and Mentoring with other Middle Management Responsibilities

Middle managers are busy people. There is a risk that if we ask them to be coaches and mentors, that they will resist this. They might see such things as additional to their middle management responsibilities and not an integral part of them. We must consider both capacity and capability at middle management level to make coaching and mentoring by them work better.

A clear understanding of why middle managers should be coaching and mentoring is needed. It should be linked as much as possible to the vision and values of the organisation. Consider how the organisation will be in the medium to long-term, and what skills – and what people – will be important in the journey to that point. What organisational problem or issues might middle manager coaching and mentoring solve?

There is no substitute for role modelling. No amount of training is as powerful as observing or experiencing senior leaders demonstrating effective coaching and mentoring. Middle managers will look to their senior leaders for cues to follow. If senior leaders themselves are displaying coaching behaviour and acting as mentors – whether that is directly to middle managers or not – the middle managers will follow. For the same reason, senior leaders should visibly celebrate the value of coaching and mentoring by middle managers. We should consider all the ways in which senior leaders (and others in the organisation) will help middle managers to be better coaches and mentors.

A strong internal community of practice for the middle managers to help them with coaching and mentoring would be a source of help too. They need to be able to compare practices, share concerns, work together to overcome barriers, and swap success stories. This community would also ensure that middle managers seek and receive feedback on their coaching and mentoring behaviours and practices to help them improve further.

A good range of development methods and resources would help middle managers become more comfortable with the roles they must play. Training programmes will be amongst those methods, but supervision-type arrangements (or having their own coach/mentor), self-study resources, use of the community of practice, and more would all be of benefit. Middle managers should be encouraged to create their own content based on where they see the pain points are in their coaching and mentoring practices too.

Building coaching and mentoring expectations and outcomes into middle manager performance management processes, and into reward and recognition processes, would help to embed the practices. Financial and time support would both be helpful but may not be immediately achievable. However, including discussions about the impact of middle management coaching and mentoring in appraisal-type discussions and publicly recognising those who do it well are likely to help.

But it may be worth starting small. If there could be barriers to making middle management coaching and mentoring work on a larger scale, no-one ever said that it all had to happen straight away. Picking a few middle managers who would be naturally good at such things would allow for them to generate some quick wins and early successes, and publicising those could help such behaviours and mindsets to spread, virally, amongst their peer groups. To help with other barriers, it would be worth these early success stories highlighting that coaching and mentoring don't have to be restricted to formal, scheduled timeslots – they could share how informal interactions and posing the right questions in ad-hoc situations have benefitted all involved.

Middle managers may also benefit from greater clarity about what type of coaching and mentoring interventions could be required from them, which should be done at the outset. Middle managers need to know what each type involves, and when to use or not to use each one (since each has distinct advantages and disadvantages). Such types include:

– Directive. This could involve sharing the experiences middle managers have had so that the person on the receiving end is able to learn from them and follow any advice shared.
– Non-directive. This involves more questioning, listening, reflecting, and the withholding of advice and / or judgement. It allows the person on the receiving end to formulate their own actions.
– Blended directive and non-directive. Moving between both above styles according to the needs of the person on the receiving end and the situation at hand.
– Leaving the person alone. Sometimes the biggest impact can be had from NOT coaching or mentoring and ensuring that the person is headed in the right direction them leaving them well alone!

This summary of available interventions may help middle managers determine what type of coach or mentor they are best suited to be, and to recognise more easily the situations where each would be the most (or least) impactful. Their practices can therefore be more tailored and less awkward and may lead to more effective development for those on the receiving end.

Developing Individuals and Teams Using Coaching, Mentoring, and other Techniques

The combination of both coaching and mentoring by middle managers can be powerful to effectively develop not just their direct reports but their teams also. There are many ways to achieve this. Google did a range of pieces of research (Project Oxygen, Project Aristotle) that explored the building blocks of high performing teams. They discovered that teams consider themselves high-performing based not on results, but the culture within the team – how they plan work, solve problems, make decisions, review progress, and work with each other. They also uncovered that teams which are high performing exhibit the following characteristics:

- Psychological safety – the team will not embarrass or punish anyone for admitting a mistake, asking a question, or offering a new idea, and have spaces where team dynamics can be openly discussed
- Dependability – the team's members reliably complete quality work on time
- Clarity – the team's members all understand the expectations of their job, and how the teamwork
- Meaning – the team all find meaning in the work of the team itself
- Impact – the team can sense the results of their work
- A common vocabulary – a shared way of communicating with each other (Google re:work, no date)

And these things are all things that middle managers could build through coaching and mentoring.

We examined Diane Allton's approach as a middle manager in Chapter 4, where she spoke about her role in a leading UK charitable organisation. I also asked her about her role developing teams and for this she gave examples of working within the healthcare sector in the UK.

When Allton began that position, she noticed that lots of teams that she was meant to support had had to deal with lots of changes during the since the Covid-19 pandemic. Demand for their services had increased significantly and many team members were worn out. It was a time of significant change, and they had to prioritise tactical work rather than having time to focus on wider organisational issues. She also saw there was a need to develop confidence levels of many first line and middle managers leading teams.

In Allton's work, she focuses on helping to encourage team spirit, with individuals exploring what it takes to become "good team members." This includes offsite work with middle managers and their direct reports. During these offsite activities she helps participants to set up their working agreements, explore their ways of dealing with conflict, and to solve problems together. These things help them be more effective as teams. The sessions also allow middle managers and their direct reports to get to know each other on a human level which helps to build a climate of trust and support.

In the example above we see how when conscious effort is made to help middle managers build teams, it can reap rewards. Interestingly, in Google's work, one of the things that had no effect on team performance was the co-location of its members – something we will explore in more depth in our next chapter.

Looking at similar aspects, Gallup also researched elements of high performing teams:
- manager talent
- playing to team members' strengths
- meaningful coaching conversations
- frequency of recognition

- leadership training
- setting motivational goals
- ongoing development (Clifton and Harter, 2019)

Once again, these are closely related to middle managers ability and willingness to be a coach and a mentor. Middle managers can help their direct reports and teams to know themselves better, gain clarity on individual and team goals, understand expectations about how to work, and behave and communicate within their teams, solve problems, and resolve conflicts more effectively. Gallup discovered that the manager accounts for 70% of the variance in team engagement – that the best managers have regular, meaningful coaching conversations with their teams (Clifton and Harter, 2019). This means that the middle managers will ask lots of questions, elicit input from their direct reports and teams, give them feedback, provide support and guidance, facilitate problem solving and conflict resolution, and encourage recognition amongst the teams.

Karen Dolan has been a middle manager in large organisations, managing geographically dispersed teams as well as different sub-cultures across the world. She spoke to me about her experiences of doing this. These experiences pre-dated the explosion in remote working that came from the Covid-19 pandemic, and Dolan's teams were almost entirely virtual.

Dolan felt it was important to spend time talking to her direct reports at times that worked for them, and not her. She asked each direct report to pick the best time for her to catch up with them and stuck with that even if time-zones made that trickier. This enabled her to clarify her expectations of each of her direct reports, and vice versa. Dolan created individual management arrangements using this approach.

Dolan also felt that those working without any geographically close colleagues could feel isolated within the team, so buddied people up to foster closer relationships, the sharing of knowledge and to mitigate risks if anyone moved on. This was supported by an annual 3-day in-person conference where there was a lot of relationship building and team development. The result of these activities was the creation of quasi-community of practice amongst her teams and direct reports, where each person understood the role of the team, their role within it, and how they could support each other. Everyone was encouraged to share their views of how they could work better with others in the wider team using a Stop/Start/Continue framework.

Dolan's team were globally dispersed and yet, in her view, could communicate and collaborate with each other better than some teams who were all co-located. She feels that agreeing expectations, clarifying accountabilities and responsibilities were key to this. In working with her direct reports, she encouraged them to manage their own teams by focusing not just on performance issues but the human aspects of work too – asking her managers to ask what they can do for their own teams and how they can get to know their teams better.

In the above example, Dolan was a coaching and mentoring manager in line with research collated by Google and Gallup. She ensured that through the right application of coaching and mentoring skills that she was able to develop her direct reports and her teams as a middle manager. But what intrinsic motivation is there for middle managers to do this, and what tools and techniques could help them?

Helping Middle Managers To Be Better Coaches and Mentors to Develop Their Teams

Given the research shared so far, it seems obvious that middle managers could get some rewards from being coaches and mentors to their direct reports and teams. We will underline this in this section by examining the concept of "Learnership" in middle management (a concept explored in more depth in Chapter 8) as a way of establishing intrinsic motivation for change. We will also explore a selection of relevant tools and techniques that middle managers could use when acting as a coach or a mentor.

Learnership

This concept was introduced by Ed Monk (CEO, Learning and Performance Institute) and will feature more in Chapter 8, since it covers how managers need to focus on learning as a way of achieving higher performance levels from both them and their direct reports and teams. It is based on the belief that success as a middle manager is increasingly determined by one's ability to learn, adapt and respond to the complexities of an ever-changing world (Monk, 2025). This means that being a middle manager in the modern world of work requires not necessarily a static body of knowledge or an established skillset, but a mindset that allows that manager to continuously acquire new knowledge and skills but also to share that and promote the acquisition of new knowledge and skills within their direct reports and teams. Monk asserts that if a culture of continuous learning is in place within a middle managers' area of influence, then it will be able to adapt more rapidly to a range of disruptions, and remain agile – teams solving complex problems, able to innovate at pace, and quickly pivot if required (Monk, 2025). As we have explored, this is highly likely to result in greater engagement, lower turnover and higher levels of motivation and productivity within teams.

Coaching and mentoring within middle management are key attributes to developing Learnership. An effective coaching and mentoring middle manager will have the view that they do not have all the answers, but have the right questions. They will not have a fixed mindset about ways of working but will embrace ideas and challenge assumptions. They will learn from mistakes and encourage others to do the same to continuously improve. The coaching and mentoring middle manager will ensure that all their direct reports and teams integrate such activities into their daily practices and share knowledge and learning across teams. But what tools and techniques would help them to do these things?

Tools and Techniques

There are various tools and techniques that middle managers could utilise to aid their coaching and mentoring practices, and to help them develop their direct reports and teams more effectively. The examples below are not exhaustive, but indicative of the types of tools and techniques that could be useful:

- GROW or a similar coaching model is useful for a middle manager to have in their mind when coaching either as a planned intervention or in an ad-hoc conversation. It requires the coach to help the coachee to clearly establish what it is they want to achieve from the conversation and about the specific issue being discussed. It then moves to gaining clarity about the current situation as it is and exploring reactions to it and other perceptions. The middle manager is well-placed to explore options for action with the coachee, to get them to consider what routes are available and what the coachee thinks about those, before helping the coachee to commit to action. GROW is a well-known model that many will be familiar with, but a more ad-hoc in the moment variation of it would be to consider three main questions: What is the situation? What options do you have? What will you do?
- Personality profiling tools, whether individual- or team-based, would be helpful in giving team members a common language and understanding of how teams work. It would make people more aware of their own blind spots and what they (and others) bring to the team and improve both collaboration and communication. There are many such tools, but all will offer something in this regard. Gallup's research suggests that knowing each other's strengths is more important than which strengths a team has in terms of leading to higher levels of performance. It would also enable the middle manager to tailor their coaching and mentoring approaches more effectively, and to look at the overall dynamics of the teams they are responsible for.
- Using data and using tools to analyse that data such as generative AI or Power BI, would enable the middle manager to gain greater insights into performance and to correlate trends and patterns across their teams. It would also provide them with a greater evidence base on which to have conversations about team performance.

- A framework to structure and deliver feedback such as Situation; Behaviour; Impact (SBI) may help the middle manager to prepare for and have more effective difficult conversations, which are often a feature of both coaching and mentoring conversations.
- Team Charters (or variations of this) would help the middle manager to consider how their direct reports and teams work together and relate to each other. The middle manager should be leading the discussions that create the headings for these Charters and should be examining the output from them to look at whether these will aid or hinder collaboration and communication across their various teams.
- Tools that facilitate collaboration in hybrid or remote settings such as Slack, Trello, Teams, Monday.com would each help to look at how teams are performing and what issues may be causing difficulties in collaboration and communication. With remote and hybrid working being increasingly common this can pose difficulties for middle managers to have the right "visibility" of what their teams are doing – and whilst some helpful tools are signposted here, there will be more discussion of the issues around this in our next chapter.

Case Studies

Megan Yawor is the Employee Experience Manager at Knight Frank, a global real estate consultancy with 20,000 employees worldwide. Yawor is based in the London office and was initially recruited for a newly created role as Knight Frank's Digital Learning Manager. A little over a year later, after gaining a strong understanding of the organisational culture, she became the company's first Employee Experience Manager, leading a newly established team.

When Yawor first joined her company as Digital Learning Manager, she conducted a 360-degree review of the team's purpose, performance, and perception, both with the immediate members and more broadly across the organisation. This involved understanding what they were doing, how they delivered their work, how they saw themselves and then how they were perceived. From this, she developed a strategy to raise the team's profile, improve quality and speed of delivery, introduce clearer processes, and position them as a stronger, more visible strategic partner.

Later, as she stepped into her Employee Experience Manager role, Yawor found herself building a brand-new function while simultaneously delivering on major system transformation project. With the team still forming and the scope of their work not yet fully defined, she had to quickly recruit, onboard, and mobilise her new team to support the rollout, all while juggling business-as-usual demands. Despite limited time and clarity, she was determined to define the team's purpose, understand how it was perceived, identify its opportunities for growth, and build a shared vision grounded in both the team's strengths and the organisation's evolving needs.

She was conscious that, whilst she had her own thoughts and feelings about such matters, the manager of the team should not dictate views to the team and should instead let the team explore their own views first. Yawor set up an offsite workshop to allow the team time and space to work through these important questions. The main output from this workshop was a Team Handbook. This contained elements such as the team vision, its elevator pitch, clarity on what the team does and does not do, its success measures, how its members want to feel and behave, and a partnership philosophy and framework. From this the team, facilitated by Yawor, began to explore key activities, bodies of work, and processes that flowed from the elements laid out in the Handbook.

The Handbook saw several iterations, shaped not only by the offsite activities, which included a mix of digital and physical, synchronous, and asynchronous tools, but also by employee feedback and broader business objectives. It enabled Yawor and the team to have absolute clarity on who they were as a function and what they could offer to the organisation.

Yawor ensures that any new starters joining the team are given time and space to review the Handbook and query its contents. She then uses the Handbook and individual reactions to it to personalise her management approach with each employee and the wider team – empowering her people to work in ways that suit them, whilst adopting various levels of supervision based on their varying needs. She has also been able to replicate similar approaches with each team that she is responsible for, and to standardise practices across those teams so that they work and communicate in similar ways.

Yawor's advice on building teams as a middle manager is simple and clear: listen, avoid assumptions, understand what works and what doesn't, and bring your team along with you on the journey. When I asked what makes a good middle manager, she emphasised that it's someone who serves their people, putting their team's needs ahead of their own. A good middle manager, to Yawor, creates space for others to grow and learn, advocates for their team when needed, and holds up a mirror to help individuals reflect on their decisions, practices, and behaviours. They check in regularly with direct reports and are both prepared for, and to some degree expect a wide range of personal and professional issues to come their way.

Case Study Reflections

In the above case study from Knight Frank, the following points stand out for further reflection:

– To make their teams more effective, middle managers will need to ensure that those teams take a step back from daily activities to review what they should be doing and how they should be working

– Middle managers will undoubtedly have strong views on what their teams should be doing, but should refrain from sharing those views too early – giving the teams a chance to co-create their own ways of working first

– It is helpful if middle managers create the structure for teams to work through – and help the teams to flesh out the content under each heading in the structure

– Middle managers should utilise a range of techniques and mediums to enable all team members to contribute to the discussion, and give numerous opportunities to iterate the output of the discussions

– It is important for new starters to be properly oriented with the nature of the team, and a Handbook (or similar) is a particularly effective way of achieving that and reviewing the current ways of working of the team – ensuring that it remains a live document

– A middle manager could, and should, replicate the approach across each of their teams, so that consistency and standardisation can be developed and encouraged

Action Plan

If you want to help middle managers to develop teams and utilise their skills and perspectives to best effect in developing both individuals and teams, the following questions are helpful to reflect upon:

– How will you build an understanding and commitment amongst your middle managers of why they would benefit from doing coaching and mentoring?

– How can you leverage the cross-organisational benefits of middle managers coaching and mentoring through the design of such initiatives?

– How will you model coaching and mentoring with middle managers when they question whether they have the time to coach and mentor?

– What is your ask of senior leadership at your organisation to visibly promote and encourage coaching and mentoring by middle managers? How will they recognise it?

- What form will a community of practice for middle managers to share coaching and mentoring practices take? What is the best way to get started?
- What learning resources and methods will help to develop middle managers coaching and mentoring?
- If you had to pick a pilot to generate some quick wins, who would be involved in that?
- How will you build focus on high-performing teams being an outcome from middle managers coaching and mentoring?
- What is your part in developing a culture of continuous learning and Learnership in the organisation?
- What tools and techniques will help your middle managers confidence and competence in coaching and mentoring more effectively?

References

Ahrens, J; McCarthy, G and Milner, T (2018) *Training for the coaching leader: How organizations can support managers*. Available at: https://ro.uow.edu.au/gsbpapers/524

Gallup (no date) *The science of teams – Gallup*. Available at: https://www.gallup.com/workplace/650156/science-of-high-performing-teams.aspx

Google re:work (no date) *Understand team effectiveness*. Available at: https://rework.withgoogle.com/en/guides/understanding-team-effectiveness

Ibarra, H. and Scoular, A. (2019) *The leader as coach, Harvard Business Review*. Available at: https://hbr.org/2019/11/the-leader-as-coach

MindTools (2024) *Building Better Managers*. Available at: https://www.mindtools.com/thought-leadership/reports/building-better-managers/

Monk, E. (2025) *Learnership: The Quiet Revolution in Leadership*. Available at: https://www.linkedin.com/pulse/learnership-quiet-revolution-leadership-edmund-monk-flpi–xy4me/

Reeves, M. (2024) *6 benefits of mentoring in the 2023 workplace, Forbes*. Available at: https://www.forbes.com/councils/forbeshumanresourcescouncil/2023/10/06/6-benefits-of-mentoring-in-the-2023-workplace/

Chapter Seven
Mastering Hybrid Work – Leading From Anywhere

The modern world of work can be a strange place, but it is one that middle managers must quickly grasp if they want to have the impact that we know they can have. Hybrid working is a common model in modern organisations, but one that poses challenges for middle (and other) managers alike. Collaboration can be more complicated, and inclusion harder to achieve. Productivity can be measured in diverse ways with remote and hybrid working, as can performance. Teams and individuals must be managed using new and different tools and techniques, and there are new skills and behaviours for middle managers to learn. Yet if middle managers can master the complexities of hybrid working, they really could lead from anywhere.

The Challenges that Remote and Hybrid Working Pose for Middle Managers

Hybrid working is not the same as in-person working, nor the same as remote working. Each type of approach requires some of the same skills and behaviours from middle managers, but some that are unique to the specific approach. What made someone a great middle manager in a face-to-face environment is not necessarily going to mean they are a great middle manager in a remote or hybrid environment. Unlearning and relearning skills and behaviours will help middle managers to ensure inclusive approaches across their various teams, manage effective communication, and enhance, rather than destroy, collaboration. They will also be able to more effectively manage performance without micromanaging or losing the trust of their direct reports and teams. But this isn't always the case and often too much is left to chance.

Sam spoke to me about their time as a middle manager in a hybrid organisation. The organisation in question operated in the research and development sector and employed around 1,000 people based mostly in the UK. Sam requested anonymity due to the level of criticism they were levelling at the organisation.

In the organisation middle managers were simply expected to be able to manage hybrid teams but without any guidance being given to them on how to do that, and no consistency being encouraged across the middle management population. Sam felt isolated and believes other middle managers felt the same. Many middle managers at the organisation had strong technical, but little man-

https://doi.org/10.1515/9783111713526-007

agement, skills. Sam received no development as a middle manager – he was expected to learn on the job. Whilst they did access some formal development, this was self-identified and self-funded.

The situation was made worse because the organisation wasn't really set up for remote and hybrid working and had not provided the right equipment, technology, or support for anyone who needed to do it. And the nature of new work being done in the organisation meant that hybrid working was the most appropriate approach regardless of what had been done before.

Sam had experience in a previous organisation of building a remote-first team during the Covid-19 pandemic, so considered themselves more fortunate than other middle managers. In that organisation they had consciously reset their team and worked with them to establish guiding principles for remote and hybrid working – like team charters discussed in this chapter. So, in this organisation, they repeated what had worked in the first organisation. This included dedicated channels for distinct types of communication and ensuring that individuals had sufficient connections to each other and to the team's purpose.

Sam believes that the nature of middle management means that it can be more hybrid because a lot of what they do can be done through a screen. However, they note that middle managers must be good at spotting and switching contexts, since everyone could present them with different issues and situations. Sam believes that the key – core – skills for middle managers in a hybrid world are tolerance; understanding; reframing what productivity is; being deliberate and intentional about their actions; and not leaving things to chance.

In the example above we see how middle managers in one organisation were left to "sink or swim." This is often because organisations are not fully clear on the challenges that middle managers face in a remote or hybrid environment. And this should not be the case, because of how different middle management is in a remote and hybrid environment.

I often explain face to face management as a very sensory experience. Man agers can see and hear (and, if they get close enough, even smell) what their team are doing. But in a remote or hybrid environment there is a sensory loss. This brings with it all the emotions and uncertainties that often accompany such loss. Much like with a sensory loss though adapting one's practices, unlearning, and relearning skills can be a way through such uncertainty, and managers who are used to face to face management must do precisely that.

I have found that newer managers, who have become so since the Covid-19 pandemic, often feel more comfortable than those who were managers prior to that pandemic. For those newer managers, the challenge may be simpler – learning about remote and hybrid management is all they have ever known. It is management to them, with nothing to unlearn. But the rest may be struggling, understandably. It can be hard for a leader, used to being around their direct reports and teams and using multiple senses to discern things about them, suddenly being deprived of much of the information they have relied upon to make judgements about performance, productivity, and engagement.

And the struggle is real. Research from Microsoft suggests that:

- 85% of managers say that the shift to hybrid work has made it challenging to have confidence that employees are being productive
- 12% of managers believe their hybrid teams are productive, compared to 87% of employees in those teams who feel they are productive (Microsoft, 2022, cited in Cookson, 2025)

This underlines how difficult many middle managers can find remote and hybrid working, despite lots of evidence that shows that such approaches can be significantly beneficial to all parties if carefully planned and implemented. But therein lies the challenge. Implementing a hybrid working approach is the tip of the iceberg but many organisations stop there, imagining that allowing employees to work remotely for some days a week and be onsite for the rest is all they need to do. It isn't – lots can go wrong if middle managers aren't switched on to what is required, and don't do what they are needed to do.

Information can get lost in a confusing array of communication mediums and channels. A plethora of software to use can sow confusion, and hinder collaboration. Lack of quality in-person time with colleagues can foster isolation, and teams doing their own things can lead to silo working. Managers who are used to being the hub around which onsite working takes place may prioritise and give more attention (and recognition) to those who they are co-located with and overlook the contributions of those who are remote to them for part or all the week. Middle managers can also feel isolated if they don't come into regular contact with their peers, and this can weaken cross-organisational ties and culture.

Middle managers need to examine which practices they need to let go of in the new world of work, which they need to adapt to work more effectively, and which practices they need to begin doing because of the greater significance they could hold. If they do not, they could default to "copying and pasting" things that worked in a mostly in-person environment into a remote or hybrid environment, without realising the unique nature of that new world of work.

Things like remote and hybrid working are no longer viewed as perks or rewards that can be granted or removed at will, but non-negotiable elements of the employee experience. The ability to better integrate work and life and achieve a personal sense of balance is critical to be able to attract and retain the best talent. Middle managers must ensure that these things are reflected in the reality of working in the organisation, not just buzzword values on the website. This requires a different mindset from middle managers.

We examined Meg Gorman's experiences of emotional intelligence in middle managers in Chapter 5. Gorman also spoke to me about her work as a middle manager in managing globally dispersed teams involving multiple time-zones and a reliance on remote working.

Gorman's approach was to treat every direct report and their team differently, and to work with them to explore the most efficient and effective working arrangements. She recognised that this would mean different things to different people. She helped her teams to implement asynchronous working given that the time-zones made synchronous working difficult, and to use the available technology to best effect.

Gorman promoted collaboration rather than competition across her teams, and this flowed into how her teams behaved when working onsite – ensuring that onsite working aided rather than hindered collaboration. As a middle manager Gorman was empowered to make these things work and was accountable for how it worked – which helped her to identify the middle management behaviours that supported hybrid working – human-centred leadership and focusing on how to get the best from each person.

In the example above we see how intentionality from middle managers pays dividends, and how personalising the management relationship is helpful too. This requires middle managers to have the right mindset, but also the right level of empowerment. But middle managers could also be trying to reconcile the needs of their team with the views held by senior leaders in some organisations that only onsite working will work. Microsoft examined this and found that 35% of managers had no personal preference about how often employees came onsite but felt that they had to follow company policy regardless (Microsoft, 2021, cited in Cookson, 2025). Middle managers must ensure that if they must get their hybrid employees to come onsite that there is purpose to this – connecting people to each other and showing them how to keep connections going digitally. This will be needed regardless of what the managers may feel about remote and hybrid working, or about the approach taken by their organisation. As we will see in the case study for this chapter, giving middle managers responsibility to determining what the onsite experience looks and feels like can be a useful piece of empowerment for them. It will encourage them to be more intentional and purposeful in how the onsite experience is crafted for those involved, and gain clarity on middle management actions in driving the right culture for the hybrid organisation.

And there are simple changes that middle managers could use to enable the right culture for hybrid working. For example, middle managers could more fully grasp what asynchronous working offers to their teams. Holding out for meetings seems unnecessary when group chats, and other collaborative methods, could achieve similar outcomes without the impact of bringing people synchronously together. Modern technologies could enable such asynchronous working, but middle managers need to be comfortable with using and promoting these. Many are not.

This is a true mindset shift. From the work of the team only (or best) being done when onsite, to distributed work that uses technology and asynchronous working to ensure work is done where and when it is best to do so. From only using sensory data, to using wider forms of data and evidence. From leaving the development of their direct reports and teams to chance, to focusing on closing skill gaps and anticipating future skills needs. From soft (or smart) skills being seen as nice-to-haves, to being critical game-changers for middle management.

In my book *Making Hybrid Working Work*, I state:

"Those in management positions in a hybrid working organisation could be fine with no support. They could adapt on their own and thrive. They could be lucky and have the right skillset and mindset to be able to be effective hybrid managers. But what if they aren't fine, can't adapt or thrive, and aren't lucky enough to have the right skillset and mindset? Is this something that any organisation wants to leave to chance? I suspect not. As with all other aspects of hybrid working, we must be intentional, conscious, and deliberate about the way we approach management development. If we are serious about making hybrid working work, then the key people to develop will be managers, as they could make or break the overall approach." (Cookson, 2025)

I stand by this quote and believe that the best way to achieve this level of confidence and competence for middle managers is to reboot their development as managers and leaders. The learning, the skills and knowledge and the mindsets, that anyone who became a manager when onsite management was the only choice they had, are out of date. They will no longer be right for a hybrid working organisation. Middle managers need a reset.

Fostering Collaboration and Enhancing Inclusion in a Hybrid Working Environment

One of the most common criticisms of hybrid working is that it can negatively impact both collaboration and inclusion. It could, but there is no causal link between hybrid working and those aspects. Many organisations make it work by putting in the right effort and giving the right things the right level of attention. As mentioned already in this chapter, intentionality is key. Middle managers have a crucial role to play in preventing individual and team silos from forming by establishing clear expectations around communication and asynchronous/synchronous working. They are responsible for making sure that participation is enhanced by hybrid working and that no groups are excluded and ensuring that team-bonding and relationship-building takes place between their direct reports and across their various teams.

Those leaders who feel that being onsite is a key influencer on how their employees feel and interact are correct, but the context for this and the amount of time needed to achieve the gains they want potentially have no specific number to work towards. Some organisations I have worked with achieve more collaboration and inclusion from one well-planned, well-executed onsite day per quarter, than others achieve from four mandated onsite days per week.

But a CIPD report showed 36% of organisations struggled with reduced interactions and collaboration because of hybrid working. However, they also discovered that 43% found that hybrid work improved those things (CIPD, 2020, cited in Cookson, 2025). Some organisations have clearly made it work, and others have not. The difference is the effort that is put into it.

Middle managers must ensure that if they must get their hybrid employees to come onsite that there is purpose to it. An onsite employee experience must connect employees to each other – ensuring that such connections are intentional and not random. Managers should also remind employees of ways to keep connections going digitally in between the onsite time. Collaboration and inclusion can be enhanced in a hybrid working environment, but what do middle managers need to do to make this inevitable?

Fostering Collaboration

To reduce the risk of teams working in their own silo on things that have little obvious organisational benefit, middle managers could create both a "Do" and "Don't Do" list that showcases organisational priorities, and how team activities contribute (or do not contribute) to those priorities. They could then work with their teams to identify tasks that could stop, and tasks that could improve collaboration on important organisational priorities.

To reduce the risk of individuals getting bogged down by transactional tasks that don't involve close working with other people, middle managers could examine where automation and artificial intelligence could reduce time taken on such tasks and direct their reports and teams to cross-functional tasks instead.

To improve communication flow, middle managers could, using AI or system-generated reports, analyse volume of traffic, type of communication, chosen platform, frequency, and duration of use, and more. Analysing available data about who communicates to whom, and the impact this has, could uncover useful information about team dynamics, individual training needs and where coaching conversations could be used best. It might also show the middle manager where more teambuilding or collaborative opportunities could be created based on where the communication flow is most impacted.

Middle managers can also cut through the potential noise around multiple communication tools and channels by working with their teams to establish clear guidelines on what tool/channel is to be used for what purpose. This could also include guidance on when a decision needs to be made synchronously via a meeting, or when asynchronous tools could be more effectively used.

Some may not fully grasp what asynchronous working offers to their team, but they need to do so to make hybrid working work better. Holding out for meetings seems unnecessary when group chats, and other collaborative methods, could get the team to the same place without physically needing to be in the same place. Middle managers should be comfortable in promoting and encouraging this style of working, with the technology that goes with it. Having a knowledge management bank where teams can generate their own content based on where their pain points and bottlenecks is something a middle manager could put in place to be the go-to source of information for decisions if synchronous communication isn't possible. The user-generated content could link back to its creator and show their preferred methods of communication and times/locations of working, including how to arrange to spend time with them. The middle manager should make it clear which team activities and tasks are best tackled synchronously, and which asynchronously, to minimise frustration, bottlenecks in processes, and isolation.

To minimise the risk of cross-organisational collaboration, middle managers could take responsibility for organising the socialisation elements of onsite working and creating cross-organisational project or special interest groups. They could do this virtually too, creating spaces and channels where their teams can connect on a personal level.

Enhancing Inclusion

Middle managers should seek data on the inclusion impacts of hybrid working. This could range from a simple tally chart showing the number of interactions they have with their direct reports and teams each week and analysing the patterns that emerge from that, to seeking feedback on potential or actual inclusion/ accessibility issues and perceived inequity. Evidence could also be examined of which teams have greater access to learning opportunities and sharing of knowledge and whether this is affected by work location. Hybrid working could enhance inclusion, but could also wreck it, so evidence is key to making it work.

Working out team norms such as individual check-ins with managers and as part of team meetings will ensure equal access and opportunity to raise issues and concerns, regardless of work location. Working out the cadence, and most appropriate logistics, for meetings with direct reports and their teams, is important in assessing ability to access information and colleagues, and inclusion in communication networks. Middle managers could ensure that, when it is impossible to accommodate everyone all the time, that arrangements are suitably varied so that all can attend and are equally considered.

A greater understanding of the strengths of each of their direct reports and those within their teams, as covered in previous chapters, will enable middle managers to reflect on the best ways for any individual to be involved in cross-departmental work. It may also help the middle manager to identify if any specific tasks could be delegated to them to provide growth opportunities. The knowledge that the middle manager then has about each individual and their strengths should ensure that opportunities to get involved in or be responsible for these types of work will be considered on who is best placed to do it, rather than who is physically closest to the middle manager.

The middle manager could let all their direct reports and teams know when and how they can contact them for ad-hoc chats and queries, and what to do if any of the parties works irregular hours so that the opportunity is not lost for communication. When planning more formal check-ins, the middle manager should ensure that their direct reports and teams are up to speed with important communications and have the same opportunity to respond and feedback their views, regardless of location of work.

Using Technology and Data to Manage Hybrid Teams

Middle managers have a fantastic opportunity to enhance how their direct reports and teams are managed, using new and developing technologies. Project management tools, communication platforms, and analytical tools could all help. But remembering points made in earlier chapters, we must guard against letting automation and artificial intelligence do too much, since it should not replace those middle management responsibilities that are best done by a human – coaching, mentoring, and more. The rest, though, can usually be done more easily through a screen and using digital solutions. Such technologies can improve the hybrid working, since there are many tools and platforms that enhance communication, collaboration, and feedback. There is, though, potential for teams to feel overwhelmed by too much modern technology, so middle managers must balance its introduction and use, and ensure that it enhances what teams do.

And artificial intelligence is likely to be able to help middle managers in many cases. It will reshape many jobs and functions, so middle managers must become comfortable with it and use it to examine efficiency, explore innovation, and aid decision-making. They should be open and transparent about their experiments in doing so, so that their direct reports and teams can feel and will be included in developments. A good example of balanced introduction and use of

AI by middle managers, addressing the point about potential overwhelm, is to use AI to streamline workflows and productivity, freeing up time for all concerns to do more human-centred tasks.

But what the technology enables middle managers to do is have access to more data and more effective ways of managing their hybrid teams. A remote or hybrid worker generates many more data points than an onsite worker since every digital interaction between a hybrid worker and the organisation generates potential data to look at. This is mostly digital data, compared to sensory data for face-to-face interactions. Few managers are aware of these data or know where to find them (since they are spread across multiple systems), or how to use them. This is an area where we can create middle manager impact by helping them to do this.

Earlier in this chapter we explored how middle managers could use data from communication platforms to analyse collaboration and communication across hybrid teams. Here is some other data that is available for middle managers to use with their hybrid teams:

- Data on working habits, even if aggregated and anonymised, would be useful in learning health concerns and optimising productive time. In-app tools can show working hours distribution, effectiveness of time of communication, and the impact of healthy or unhealthy working practices.
- Employee monitoring tools could give information, tracking, analysing, and reporting on employee activities during or outside working hours. Used in one way they supply surveillance data but used in other ways they can supply insights about productivity and well-being also. This can be done by tracking behavioural data – application usage, working times, browsing patterns and more to understand more about the hybrid working experience. It could allow more insight into bottlenecks, pain points, inefficiencies as well as the emotional state and health of the hybrid employee.
- Data will also be available about how often employees are onsite, where they work when they are onsite, and what resources and equipment they use. Combining this with some of the insight from monitoring tools could show some interesting patterns and trends, showing when and where peak collaboration happens. Looking at the same data for when employees are remote and analysing server and app usage could show where and when peak focused work happens too.
- All this data could be correlated with data that exists within HR or L&D systems to provide further analysis – are the patterns happening in certain teams, or to employees with certain characteristics? Are the patterns restricted to new starters or to those with particular hybrid patterns? Are the

pain points where employees are obviously seeking out support matched by use of available learning and training methods? (Cookson, 2025)

Middle managers are likely to need help and support in becoming comfortable and competent in managing their hybrid teams using these data. Regardless, they need to know what technology the organisation supplies for hybrid teams and for what purpose, what the advantages and limitations of this technology is, and what the level of digital literacy is in their hybrid teams.

Maintaining Productivity and Accountability in Hybrid Working

There can often be a perceived challenge in remote and hybrid work settings that productivity and accountability are harder to assess due to the lack of face-to-face, sensory, input that could help middle managers to do this. As explored in the section above, there is more data available than we first think, but middle managers must still set clear deliverables and timelines for tasks, conduct regular check-ins, address challenges, and provide the right balance of autonomy and support. Hybrid working can lend itself well to these things, if done right.

If teams are still managed on inputs – where they sit, how long they work for – then we are missing a trick. If workplaces are still comprised of traditional command-and-control, top-down leadership styles then we are further behind. A dispersed, flexible work environment has little place for micromanagement, lack of trust and minimal empowerment. And yet that traditional environment is still one that is common in many organisations, with middle managers desiring to control what their direct reports and teams do. This contrasts with a desire for autonomy from hybrid workers and teams and puts the effectiveness of hybrid working at risk.

Managing based on agreed outcomes could be a sensible way forward. It allows for negotiation instead of imposition and gives more flexibility and autonomy to teams on how to achieve those outcomes instead of their time and location being monitored closely. This kind of leadership needs more trust since middle managers won't always be co-located with their employees. This can be encouraged by creating a type of "management agreement" which sets out how each middle manager will work with each of their direct reports and teams – covering things like how each will update the other; how, when, where they will meet and what they'll cover in those meetings; performance outcomes and broad expectations on how these will be delivered; data required to get assurance about performance and what is available synchronously or asynchronously; exceptions where working arrangements may need to change; the equipment and resource needs when working at different locations; and more.

This kind of personalised working arrangements for teams is likely to help middle managers unlock productivity. Research found that what separates those who are productive anywhere from those who are disconnected and frustrated is whether they have the right resources, autonomy, work/life balance, supportive leadership, and a digitally mature organisation (Accenture, 2021). The same research showed that 63% of high-revenue growth organisations have hybrid work models where teams can choose where to work, and 69% of negative or no-growth organisations are still focused on mandating on-site working (Accenture, 2021). If these personalised team arrangements are put in place, middle managers can then focus on a light-touch approach in encouraging and maintaining healthy working practices and acting on unhealthy working practices. Some organisations do this very well indeed.

Rob Ashcroft spoke to me about his time both as a middle manager – Head of People Capability – and developing other middle managers, at a large UK-based financial institution and implementing agile working there.

Ashcroft felt that middle management at that organisation was a difficult place to be. He felt continual pressure to be accountable for the performance of his teams, but without the time and resources to do the things that would lead to greater performance – things like coaching, mentoring, encouraging, and motivating individuals and teams. At times, he and other middle managers felt that management was something "on top of the day job." In Ashcroft's case it often was – he had to work additional hours to do the value-adding activities.

Ashcroft also felt that being a middle manager was compliance-focused, ensuring that policies were strictly adhered to and with no allowance for context, situation, individual needs, or middle management preferences. When it was identified that any middle manager may have been struggling (though things like engagement survey results, or succession planning discussions), the solution was often an offsite 2–3-day training course that treated the symptom rather than the cause.

The organisation was introducing agile working principles, partly driven by efficiency concerns, but Ashcroft saw this as a tool to examine culture change and leadership behaviours at the same time. He drew on Dan Pink's Drive theory to provide some structure for examining these things and made sure that he implemented agile principles within his own team before setting his team the task of supporting other middle managers to implement their versions of agile. Other models that informed Ashcroft's approach included: Holocracy and the debate that ensues about whether management hierarchies are necessary; and the Trust Equation, focusing on how to create psychological safety in teams. This enabled Ashcroft to encourage strong governance within teams rather than strong management, and to embed individual accountabilities without management oversight. All these things worked within his own team, leading to higher engagement and productivity. Other teams became interested in adapting the agile principles for their contexts, and Ashcroft's team began to help them to do that.

Transparency was key to the success of agile working principles – the idea that everything was, or could be, "on display" – giving visibility to what each person and the whole team was doing, what performance was like for each person and how it was being managed. Ashcroft encountered some resistance from middle managers, driven by fear of not being able to manage how they were used to managing. This was overcome through social learning with other middle managers, increased communication, and discussions throughout the organisation about what the purpose of middle management was (to coach, to lead learning, to motivate and nurture their team, to drive a performance culture). This was a reimagining of what middle management was – a mindset shift as much as a new skillset. It changes what management authority is, where their power base comes from, and makes middle managers get used to not being the hub around which work revolves. Ashcroft realised that agile working wasn't for everyone – some middle managers were not ready for it and may never be. He advises being clear on middle managers roles as cultural architects, showing them the idea culture and getting them to assess their level of fit with it.

Ashcroft supported these changes with psychometric tests to look at middle managers strengths and areas for development; support on how to use data to make decisions; training on coaching skills and storytelling skills; guidance on how to use canvases for collaboration, and how to use agile-specific ways of working. When the Covid-19 pandemic arrived, the organisation was ready for that given the work that Ashcroft and his team had done to rethink what middle management was and how they and their teams could work in an agile way.

In the example above we see how rethinking the role of middle managers and how they operate with their direct reports and teams can unlock productivity and accountability, but there must be conscious effort behind this. Otherwise, middle managers may want to hold teams accountable by bringing them onsite to check their work in-person. This is unsuitable for hybrid working, but research suggests that even onsite teams only spend 36%-39% of their time working (Tsipursky, 2023). If a middle manager prioritises onsite working as a way of checking productivity and holding teams accountable, they could focus on time spent working at the onsite location instead of what really matters.

One way to ensure that this happens is for the middle managers to work with their direct reports and teams to develop their own performance measures and reporting, and to encourage the creation of digital methods to report and share this. This will allow middle managers to get a handle on productivity wherever and whenever they or their teams are working, and to hold their teams more accountable for their own-devised measures.

We might also need to help middle managers to reframe and redefine productivity. Middle managers are dealing with human beings. Their focus should be on the human being and not on the task if they are to unlock productivity. A good day for a middle manager could be how much time they have spent checking-in with their direct reports and teams, and how they have made each person feel when doing that. A good day for a hybrid employee could be something different entirely – but unless we ask them, how would we know?

Critical Leadership Behaviours for Hybrid Working

Throughout this section we have explored how the middle management role needs to change in a hybrid working environment. They must adapt to digital-first practices, demonstrate flexibility and empathy, and lead by example with effective communication and accountability. In this section we will examine some of the appropriate behaviours to achieve this. Gartner found that 84% of HR leaders felt it was more important for managers to develop soft skills in a hybrid setting (Gartner, 2021).

I agree. Those in middle management roles need to raise their game around what may previously have been termed "soft skills," but which must now be regarded as essential managerial skills for success. I am not sure the label "soft skills" gives sufficient importance to these skills, so I have begun terming them "smart skills" instead.

Those in middle management positions in a hybrid working organisation could be fine with no support. They could adapt on their own and thrive. They could be lucky and have the right skillset and mindset to be able to be effective hybrid managers. But what if they aren't fine, can't adapt or thrive, and aren't lucky enough to have the right skillset and mindset? Is this something that any organisation wants to leave to chance? If we are serious about making the new world of work work, then the key people to develop will be middle managers, as they could make or break the overall approach. I recommend rebooting leadership and management development. Managers need a reset (Cookson, 2025). And middle managers even more so.

Flexibility is an important behaviour for middle managers in a hybrid environment. This would mean approaching each situation – each team, each individual – potentially differently, but with a guiding set of principles that offer consistency whilst allowing for flexibility.

Middle managers should avoid micromanaging and focus on setting expectations and building trust with their teams through techniques explored already in this and other chapters. Personalised relationships with their direct reports and teams should take account of their needs for flexibility, their wellbeing, and give all a voice within the organisation. This would also help foster a culture where psychological safety is paramount.

From a cultural perspective, middle managers need to be comfortable communicating effectively across a wide range of potential platforms and channels and encouraging/helping others to do the same – ensuring each of their direct reports and teams are connected to other teams and the wider organisational purpose regardless of working location. They need to be accessible and available to build the personal and professional connections they need with remote and hybrid workers. They need to clearly establish with their direct reports and teams the desired culture and work to reinforce this through their behaviour with in-person and remote teams. This might involve consciously doing more apprecia-tion and recognition and providing more feedback – but also encouraging teams to do this between themselves.

As various developments, including AI and hybrid working, disrupt the way work is done, teams will need to abandon rigid, fixed roles and skillsets and be-come more dynamic in learning new tasks and roles. Because of this, middle man-agers may need to strongly encourage and facilitate the learning of new skills and ensuring that the team develop complementary skillsets and allow for replanning, rethinking, and re-engineering of work. Middle managers must model adaptabil-ity and a willingness to experiment with new tools, processes, and team struc-tures. They must champion learning and ensure that their teams have access to digital learning tools, micro-learning content, and have protected time for their own personal development. They must find time to continuously scan trends, learn, and adapt to stay relevant – and to encourage their hybrid teams to do likewise.

Middle managers need to know, amongst other things:

- What middle management tasks need performing onsite and which do not, and what makes a great hybrid middle manager
- How often they need to be co-located with their direct reports and teams, and for what purpose
- How to access support from within the organisation on managing hybrid teams
- How to use their emotional intelligence to know when to speak to, or when not to, a hybrid report or team, and what signals could help them work that out
- What the signs of unhealthy or poor working practices and wellbeing in a hybrid worker or team, and what to do to address them
- How to ensure their hybrid reports and teams understand the impact that their work has on other teams and the wider organisation – including things like missing deadlines, skipping or being late for meetings and more
- How to facilitate team development so that the hybrid team becomes high performing (Cookson, 2025)

All this means that middle management in a hybrid world of work is different. A new skillset, a new mindset. We must encourage them to grow and develop in this world and continuously thereon.

Case Studies

Sue Hughes spoke to me about her time as Director of HR & OD at Halton Housing (HH), where she worked from 2010 to 2019. HH is a social housing organisation employing several hundred people in the North of the UK. During this time HH pioneered a move to bring a digital and remote first organisation well ahead of when many others were forced to during the Covid-19 pandemic or chose to afterwards. Key to this was work Hughes and her team did with middle managers to help them to operate on a digital and remote first basis.

The driver behind the transformation was initially to reduce office locations, combining two major locations into one. At the same time, HH's Chief Executive – a digital pioneer – wanted to move the organisation to a digital-first footing so that its customers could access all their services through a screen. It was felt that both things – location change, and technology change – would deliver considerable efficiencies.

When examining the office location, Hughes and her team analysed current occupancy levels and deduced that average occupancy across the existing HH offices was around 70–75%. No new office would be able to fit more than 70% of the staff in it at any one time, and the move to digital-first services meant that office occupancy would drop significantly from its current levels due to increased remote working. These realisations meant that HH decided not to build an office large enough to accommodate everyone, since it was highly unlikely everyone would need to be accommodated simultaneously. It doubled down on its digital and remote first approach to leverage even more efficiencies.

Hughes and her team were then tasked with planning the people-related elements of these changes – which were considerable – and began planning how to support middle managers with this change. As was expected, some welcomed the change, but others did not. HH's middle management population of 55 included several what Hughes calls "traditional managers", those who looked at numbers in the office as a way of assessing productivity. HH also had a lot of newer managers, who Hughes noted were more in favour of the changes to being digital and remote first.

Hughes ensured that each manager was given individual support and built a bespoke individual support programme for each one. This helped her to accommodate unique styles, different team arrangements and a more tailored amount of support for diverse needs. This included individual coaching support for middle managers that helped them examine their own style as leaders and managers, whether that was appropriate for the new organisational vision, and how they could drive the strategic changes forward. This also helped to identify existing pockets of good practice that could be recognised and spread.

Before the coaching took place, Hughes contracted with each middle manager so that they were clear what it would cover and began the coaching three months before the changes were due to happen so that the middle management population could be more ready for supporting their direct reports and teams through the changes. Each middle manager had up to 6 coaching sessions over that 3-month period, initially delivered by Hughes and her team before capacity issues necessitated bringing in an external coach.

Whilst HH wanted to grasp this once in a generation opportunity to drive change, there were mixed responses to the coaching support. Some middle managers didn't engage with the support available to them, feeling that the coaching was "another HR initiative" rather than something intrinsically linked to the strategic changes. On reflection, Hughes wishes that HH had made the coaching sessions mandatory, since those who needed it the most refused to take part. However, for those who did take part, the coaching was successful in reinforcing the strategic direction and the preferred middle management style for a digital and remote first organisation.

Another form of support were regular Managers Forum meetings (which were mandatory for all). These lasted half a day and were discussion-based. As part of this change, HH talked to middle managers about how teams were currently managed; what their challenges were; what their opportunities were; what was working and what was not; and how their teams would change and react to the organisational changes. The Forum also covered a range of other important organisational issues.

Middle managers found the Forum beneficial. They offered a chance to network, be kept up to date on organisational issues, to reflect, to talk about appropriate leadership and management styles, and familiar challenges such as how to monitor engagement and involvement in a digital and remote first organisation. The Forum thus became a strong and cohesive Community of Practice where middle managers could share good practice (though much began to be shared informally as relationships began to strengthen). Hughes wishes that HH had devoted more time to the sharing of ideas in this formal setting and to formally capture the learning from the process. It was felt to be a hugely beneficial arrangement, but this was measured anecdotally. An early topic was how middle managers could manage based on outputs and outcomes rather than inputs, which prompted lots of helpful discussions and a few agreements on how to best do this. Middle managers also created approaches to checking in with both individuals and teams.

Hughes also gave advice to middle managers on how to bring their teams together in-person (whether onsite or at a neutral location) and to create a purpose for that – sharing, collaborating, and socialising. Most teams at HH enjoyed the move to digital and remote first working, but still craved connection with their team-mates and the wider organisation. Hughes tasked middle managers with creating purpose and structure to onsite working – encouraging them to plan these collaboratively and well in-advance, and to build a rhythm and regularity to them. Middle managers focused on socialisation and collaborative activities rather than just "working" onsite and were responsible for making the onsite working elements successful. They were helped with the new (smaller) office, which lent itself to agile working, collaboration, and socialisation – having been purposely designed with these things in mind.

Reflecting on what she and her team did at HH, Hughes is rightly proud of the achievements. She feels the support to middle managers was the right thing to do at the right time. It helped to reinforce behaviours, to define and shape teams, to improve processes and communication, to develop managers to lead better and to get to know their teams better.

Case Study Reflections

In the HH case study the following points stand out for further reflection:
– Middle managers are often key to organisational change and transformation, so investing time and effort in support for them is critical. Their inability to take part is not necessarily resistance – change cannot happen without middle management.
– Middle managers as a group will have a range of those comfortable with, and much less comfortable with, large scale organisational change
– Providing tailored individual support for middle managers is helpful in respecting their needs and preferences
– Often those who need coaching the most will not recognise this, so finding some way to encourage take-up is important
– The creation and active management of a Community of Practice is helpful in identifying and sharing good practice
– Providing middle managers with key questions, and empowering them to work up the answers and determine the approaches that all middle managers would follow, is an effective way to build engagement with digital and remote first working
– Giving middle managers specific responsibility for the onsite elements of hybrid working gave such things a purpose and sense of cohesion – a cultural dimension

Action Plan

If you want to help middle managers move to an effective hybrid approach, the following questions are worth answering:

- How can you help middle managers cope with the sensory loss that accompanies less in-person working?
- What middle management practices are unsuited to hybrid working? How will you help middle managers let go of those?
- How can you give middle managers some responsibility for making hybrid working work?
- How will you consciously reset leadership development so that middle management confidence and competence is not left to chance?
- What do middle managers need to do to create a purposeful onsite working experience for all?
- What digital communication can middle managers make use of to keep connections going in-between onsite working?
- How will you help middle managers analyse communication and collaboration data and patterns?
- What support needs to be provided to help middle managers become more comfortable with asynchronous working?
- How will middle managers check the inclusion impacts of hybrid working?
- How will artificial intelligence be used to make hybrid working work by middle managers?
- What use will be made of data that is generated about the hybrid worker experience?
- What will personalised management arrangements from middle managers look and feel like?
- How can teams develop their own performance measures?
- What content will go into a middle manager hybrid working training programme, and how will you make this work?

References

Accenture (2021) *Demographics play a role: 74% of gen zs would like more opportunities to collaborate with colleagues in a face-to-face setting.* Available at: https://newsroom.accenture.com/news/2021/a-work-anywhere-workplace-is-what-employees-actually-want-today-according-to-new-report-by-accenture

Cookson, G. (2025) *Making hybrid working work: A practical guide for business success.* London: Kogan Page.

Gartner (2021) *Gartner recommends organizations pursue three strategies to ensure managers succeed in the hybrid world*. Available at: https://www.gartner.com/en/newsroom/press-releases/2021-12-01-gartner-recommends-organizations-pursue-three-strategies-to-ensure-managers-succeed-in-the-hybrid-world

Tsipursky, G. (2023) *Five essential strategies for successful Hybrid Leadership*, *Allwork.Space*. Available at: https://allwork.space/2023/07/five-essential-strategies-for-successful-hybrid-leadership/

Chapter Eight
The Future of Middle Management

We have examined what middle managers do and how they can make a difference in their organisations. We have noted that the world of work we inhabit now is different from that of the past. It will continue to change in the future, and middle managers must be a part of this rather than observers to that change. In this chapter we explore why adaptability is a core middle management skill, and how they can foster a culture of continuous learning in their teams. We look at how middle managers can build their own resilience and growth mindset, and how they can stay relevant into the future. We conclude by advocating for life-long learning for middle managers, preparing them for whatever future comes.

Adaptability – The New Core Middle Management Skill?

In the face of rapid and near-constant organisational change, and a shifting world of work, middle managers must respond quickly and with relevance. Adaptability is the core skill for middle managers need to be able to respond and pivot accordingly. In this section we will explore why, and how.

In the world of work that we now inhabit, with change all around, if a middle manager isn't changing and consciously improving what they do, they and those they manage could well fall behind. To a large degree we can't control what life and work throws at us, but we can prepare for it, and plan different responses. We also know from previous chapters that if middle managers coach and mentor well that high engagement and performance is a likely outcome. Such high-performing teams are also likely to be the most agile, along with the middle manager to whom they report. This is important because of the emotional impact that change often has, as we explored in Chapter 4. This isn't always negative, but shaped by context and content of the change, the relationship with those leading and communicating it, the legacy of past changes, and the perception of support and fairness (CIPD, 2014). Therefore, if middle managers can demonstrate agility and responsiveness in a changing world, their teams are likely to follow suit. If middle managers are emotionally ready to change, they can help others to do the same and smooth the necessary transitions.

Emotional intelligence, as we explored in Chapter 5, is crucial for adapting to change, as it can enhance self-awareness and emotional regulation. Those aspects help middle managers to respond well to changing priorities and a shifting environment. Middle managers with elevated levels of emotional intelligence are bet-

https://doi.org/10.1515/9783111713526-008

ter equipped to handle uncertainty and ambiguity, critical traits in today's workplace (Freedman et al, 2023).

Interestingly, a study found that some middle managers consciously hid their adaptability and agile traits in some organisations, concerned that senior leaders would view preparing for unknowns and learning new skills as subversive behaviour, responding cynically to such traits (Bower, cited in Floyd and Woolridge,1994). This suggests that there is a cultural dimension to adaptability that can either encourage or discourage such efforts, meaning we must be careful how we expect middle managers to demonstrate it. Middle managers often operate in highly pressured environments and must still exercise management responsibilities with their direct reports and teams even if they are being adaptable. There are many ways to be adaptable and agile, and to encourage teams reporting to middle managers to do that too, without being openly against the status quo:

– Coaching and mentoring teams should lead to exploration of different perspectives and ways of thinking within those teams, opening capacity to navigate uncertainty without incurring additional costs or requiring additional resources
– Building a habit of reflection before and after action is helpful – asking questions such as: what could I do to better understand the situation I am about to encounter? And what could I have done differently in the situation I have just left that would have led to a better outcome?
– Focusing on cross-organisational relationships, and particularly the informal, social aspects of these should help middle managers learn more about changes in other parts of the organisation that could affect them in the future, and plan more effectively for them
– Transforming routine check-ins from status updates to growth opportunities. Instead of asking "what's the status?" middle managers could try "What are you learning?" – shifting the conversation from tracking progress to building capacity (Hudson, 2025)
– Seeking out diverse experiences and people – which might expose the middle manager to different ideas and ways of thinking that they could adapt
– Looking after oneself – taking the appropriate breaks, and doing relevant physical activity in between work tasks – can maintain energy levels and overall resourcefulness for middle managers

The above is not an exhaustive list but suggests some ways to consciously and subconsciously build adaptability and agility into middle management practice.

Freya is a people professional working in the UK's Energy sector. She is also the Co-Chair of her organisation's Women's Employee Resource Group. She spoke to me about her time as a middle manager in multiple sectors and industries.

She feels that there are big gaps at middle manager level, with organisations often promoting based on technical ability with little reference to the people skills needed, and then not effectively providing the right support and development to those middle managers. She also pointed out that the average age of middle managers – in their early-forties to mid-fifties, means that they are facing the perfect storm in their personal lives too. By this she means peak mortgage debt, potential divorce, statistically more likely to have both childcare and eldercare issues and be developing their own health issues too. Because of the lack of awareness, preparation and support within organisations, and the issues faced by middle managers in their personal lives, she feels many middle managers sink under the pressure and often leave organisations, particularly women. Organisations must do more to support them and help them to grow.

Freya recommends a range of organisational support networks that middle managers can access, and which confront the elephant in the room in terms of the mix of personal and professional issues faced by most middle managers. Where she currently works there are many of these – such as working parents' groups, mid-life and mental well-being groups and more – which middle managers are often a key part of, and don't necessarily tackle the issues unique to middle management but do provide a valuable support network for them. Freya feels that this enables middle managers (and others in the groups) to bring their authentic self to work, and to examine ways in which work can become more flexible to adapt to personal challenges.

Freya feels that cohorts going through development programmes will often fulfil the same purpose. She feels that engaging middle managers as a cohort rather than as individuals allows for the entire group to be brought along on the development journey and face organisational changes and challenges collectively. When dealing with middle managers across her career she has encountered a natural split when faced with organisational change. She has seen many that are receptive to and excited about change and growth, and plenty that are the opposite.

Freya deliberately targets the resistant/reluctant middle managers to get on board with change, feeling if she can get them to experience the mental and emotional growth needed for change then that will positively influence others. She provides one to one support for middle managers and helps them to de-catastrophise issues by asking for their input and talking about the relevance of the changes. Again, the aim is to help them to grow as people and as middle managers.

Freya's most recent development programme for middle managers ensures that the cohort are comfortable with not having the right answers, but more comfortable using the right questions and listening actively to the people they work with. This helps to build their confidence and is supported by a range of other helpful development methods – mentoring for and by middle managers; reverse mentoring; peer coaching; training on dealing with difficult conversations; dealing with conflict; handling imposter syndrome; role modelling values and change; and creating an inclusive environment. The value of this programme is clearly highlighted to all middle managers and promoted to their direct reports and teams as being of high value to the middle managers too.

In the example above, we see how middle managers at National Grid are given time and space to become more adaptable and agile. Key to both though is the ability to learn.

Fostering a Culture of Continuous Learning

Lifelong or continuous learning makes a significant difference to anyone's ability to deal with the future. If middle managers can instil amongst their direct reports and teams a curiosity and desire to innovate, and a growth mindset, the teams will benefit. If middle managers can encourage ongoing skills development and provide access to and encouragement to use a range of learning resources and methods, then the teams and the organisation at large will also benefit. We will examine these in this section.

The future for organisations is to be more skills-based, where there is a clear understanding of the skills that they need to deliver on their strategic goals and individual aspirations. This is partly because the growth of artificial intelligence will disrupt work, shifting how, when and where tasks are done. It means that the skills that individuals and teams have need to be flexible enough to adapt to new or different tasks, and competitive advantage could come from being able to unlearn and relearn skills at pace. Organisations need teams that can adapt quickly, learning modern technologies and processes. By focusing on future skill requirements, organisations can equip their workforce with the precise abilities needed to swiftly and effectively adapt to evolving market demands and technological advancements – with research showing that organisations which do this are 63% more likely to achieve results than those that do not (Kapoor et al, 2025). The World Economic Forum suggests that 39% of existing skillsets will be transformed or become outdated by the end of 2030, but that 63% of employers identified skill gaps as the major barrier to business transformation (WEF, 2025). So, skills critical to the future are in short supply, and the skills that most have now won't be relevant in the future. We have a problem, and middle managers can help.

Middle managers can create an emotionally safe environment for their direct reports and teams, with high trust, an acceptance of making mistakes but learning from them, and empathy for personal situations, then this becomes a foundation for continuous learning. Middle managers can demonstrate curiosity and openness to innovative ideas and provide constructive feedback that helps teams to improve without feeling demoralised, reinforcing a learning culture. Middle managers can provide task clarity and coaching on how to achieve tasks, supporting growth and development. Middle managers can learn more about their teams' strengths and challenges, staying attuned to their evolving needs and being clear about how these strengths may need to be adapted in future. Speaking on a CIPD podcast, Wayne Clarke talked about his time working on the Sunday Times Best Companies accreditation process, and how many respondents asserted that "I've got skills that the organisation could use but doesn't" (CIPD, 2023). But a great middle manager wouldn't allow that to happen. Middle managers should be invested in their own growth and development, but also the growth and development of their direct reports and teams, so that everyone wins – but that is often left to chance by organisations. A middle managers' ability to do the things described here is not often a consideration when they are given the role, and yet it should be. They need to be equipped for the role through a range of different methods.

Anya leads management and leadership development at a large UK public sector organisation. The organisation has 3,500 staff, of whom four hundred are middle managers. She spoke to me about her focus on developing middle managers at the organisation.

Upon joining the organisation, Anya noticed two big gaps. One for new managers – there was little support in place for them and the organisation relied on their own manager to give a good induction. When a new manager did find themselves at a training course, they'd report that they'd had no induction and just been left to get on with it. There was no guidance for managers of managers, what was expected or how they should adapt to their own new role. There was the usual focus on operational delivery but little on management ability, which only tended to come under scrutiny when HR issues emerged.

Anya and the wider HR team began to implement a few changes to help middle managers (and their direct reports) to grow and develop.

– New manager inductions for both new managers and new managers of managers – both a workshop and an induction guide
– A Standards and Capabilities Framework to define the management role – at all levels – better.
– An annual 180 feedback mechanism for all managers, with coaching support to reflect on feedback received and decide actions – coaching is delivered by a pool of internal feedback coaches.
– Informal Communities of Practice – existing both digitally through email and internal social media channels – and face-to-face.
– An expectation that all managers had a line management objective as well as delivery objectives
– Working with my company EPIC to deliver workshops on Managing Managers, aimed at clarifying what a good manager is and how a manager of managers can work with their direct reports to ensure that they are doing what the organisation needs them to do and accessing the support they need.

For the future, Anya has a focus on redoing some of the "manager fundamentals," broadening the range of topics and resources available. She wants to build advanced learning for middle and senior managers relevant to the realities of their role which includes team leadership, understanding of systems thinking, stakeholder engagement and influencing skills.

In the example above, we see how an organisation can improve the capabilities of middle management through learning. My own involvement in that example includes a focus on how middle managers can help their direct reports to learn and grow. But how do middle managers themselves achieve this growth mindset to help them prepare for the future?

Building Resilience and a Growth Mindset in Middle Managers

There are several ways in which this can be done, from using networks and communities of practice, regular reflection, and having clear aspirations.

- As mentioned already in this chapter, looking after oneself is a good starting point. Ensure that middle managers know how their resilience is connected to their physical health, and how even small improvements in sleep, nutrition and/or exercise could reap huge benefits for them
- Mental fatigue can be tackled by using distractions such as hobbies, meditation, doing puzzles and more
- Reflection, again mentioned already in this chapter, is an effective way to objectively analyse a situation and identify what situations cause stress for a middle manager, and what situations they are best able to demonstrate resilience in. This can be developed further through techniques such as journalling – the act of writing down what happened, the middle managers reaction to it, and the lessons learnt from that.
- Reframing situations – looking at them from different angles and searching for missing information – could expose a middle manager to innovative ideas and ways of tackling problems
- Practicing mindfulness techniques and positive self-talk can help mitigate unhelpful emotional reactions from middle managers and a desire to make any situation better
- Seeking feedback from others on how the middle manager has dealt with a situation and/or asking for their advice on how it could have been handled better will increase confidence in dealing with similar situations when they next occur

These methods are rooted in developing self-awareness, a key pillar of emotional intelligence – the importance of which for middle managers we noted in Chapter 5. These methods should help middle managers view situations as growth opportunities for themselves, their direct reports, and their teams. But whilst growing is important, how do middle managers ensure that they remain relevant for the future world of work?

Staying Relevant as a Middle Manager

Middle management has come under threat in many organisations. To avoid more threats, they must keep themselves up to date, grow their own skills, and stay informed about future trends and technologies. Certain middle management skills will become even more important in the new world of work, and we'll explore all of this in this section.

Artificial Intelligence and Middle Management

We know that AI will redefine what work is, where and when it is done, and how it is done. This means that tasks will change, work will change, teams will change and so will middle management. However, AI should be a major boost for middle managers if middle managers are able to harness it correctly. Middle managers don't necessarily need to know the finer detail of AI, but what they do need is to be able to motivate and coach their direct reports and teams to use the finer detail. They need to be able to facilitate the redesign and reshaping of work, keeping a higher-level view on how resources can be best distributed, and ensuring that the efficiency gains promised by AI are fully realised by the humans deploying it.

We know that some organisations feel that deploying AI correctly will lead to less need for middle managers. The opposite may well be true. Teams will still need to be led and co-ordinated. Research has shown that if middle management layers are reduced, that this creates bottlenecks for control and decision-making at the top of the organisation (Kapoor et al, 2025), which isn't helpful for anyone.

AI will increasingly perform routine administrative tasks, and greater amounts of technical and research-based tasks too. It will perform more complex tasks as the years progress. But it cannot (yet) exercise the judgement that human beings – specifically middle managers, with their unique view of and position in the organisation – can. Middle managers will better understand the organisational context, apply their emotional intelligence, and be adaptable enough to improvise in the face of changing circumstances. Middle management experiences will help them to be able to develop their judgement skills, and the emotional intelligence discussed in Chapter 5 help them to have the right level of empathy to be able to recognise what the right call is in the right situation. AI therefore removes some management tasks – the need to instruct teams on what to do and the need to manage the output from those teams – but what remains takes on far greater importance as a result.

Utilising AI to take the burden of administrative duties from middle managers could free them up to build their teams more effectively by coaching and mentoring them as explored in Chapter 6. AI could also help refine middle managers' abilities in coaching particularly by acting as the employee or team for the middle manager to practice their coaching on. It can help develop their judgement skills by giving them problems to solve and feedback on their recommended actions. And we know also that AI could help to collate and analyse data about remote and hybrid teams, as we explored in Chapter 7, giving managers real-time insights into how their direct reports and teams are performing and behaving. This allows middle managers to develop skills that AI cannot replicate, for example critical thinking, context-based decision-making, and more. Whilst this means that middle managers must keep up to date with emerging technologies, they must ensure that they evolve with the implementation of the technology – or risk being replaced by it.

Softer Skills – or Smarter Skills? Emotional Intelligence and the Middle Manager

Throughout this book I have highlighted how what we term as softer skills, but which I now call smarter skills, are much more relevant to middle managers in the modern world of work than ever before. We know from the above paragraphs that AI can free up middle management time to use more of these types of emotionally intelligent skills. Emotional intelligence can help middle managers to build stronger networks and collaborate across silos, helping them stay informed of emerging trends and shifts. Managers with high emotional intelligence are better placed to drive change and keep themselves and their teams ahead of the curve. Good levels of smarter skills help to manage the energy of other people and their commitment to organisational goals. And yet Gallup has found that organisations fail to choose the right type of middle manager for this 82% of the time (Olsen, 2022).

But if they did focus on smarter skills when recruiting middle managers, the potential benefits are there for all to see. Great middle managers can motivate their direct reports and teams and engage them with the organisational mission and vision. They can build better relationships and foster trust and accountability. Research has found that if employees are more engaged then higher performance outcomes follow (Olsen, 2022). By fostering the type of environment we have discussed in this book – where teams' growth and learning is prioritised, where decision-making happens at all levels, where teams are encouraged to unlearn and relearn skills and behaviour, to try new things and learn from that, and to challenge out-dated processes and find more efficient ways of working – middle managers can not only keep themselves relevant but their direct reports and teams also.

Middle managers must stay relevant by continually growing and developing in these two key areas, but organisations and senior leaders must play a part too.

We examined Nick Holmes' approach to middle management in Chapter 5. In his current role, Holmes has been developing middle managers for over a decade and feels that this can only be done by reflecting the real-world challenges that they have – avoiding too much theory and grounding it in practicality. Holmes builds programmes based on the pain points that middle managers have, and links to the organisational values and vision of what management should be.

The current middle management development programme Holmes is running is experiential, flexible, and includes a range of learning methods. There is a "Choose Your Own Adventure" theme that allows middle managers to pick their own route through the programme, based on four core elements (Manager Mindset; Unlocking Peak Performance; Communicating with Courage; and Making it Stick). The final element, Making it Stick, is applicable to all regardless of their routes through the other three elements. It is mostly about reflection, application of learning, group coaching, and talks from alumni.

The programme runs with twenty middle managers per cohort. Senior leaders are actively involved in delivering the programme, with strategically placed fireside chats. Guest speakers, actors, and roleplay situations are all well-received too. Whilst individuals do choose their own routes through the programme, the pre-work (including lots of pre-assessments) is standardised and provides a consistent grounding for the journey to follow. Once completed, Holmes has created an opt out for middle managers who now realise that it isn't for them, where they can become individual contributors instead. Some have opted for this, but most don't.

Holmes measures the impact of the programme by comparing the pre- and post- programme self-assessments and incorporates 360-degree feedback here too. Middle managers have six monthly career conversations which include an Impact rating that is expected to improve for both middle managers and their direct reports – and it has. The programme also measures retention rates for both middle managers and their direct reports, and this too has improved.

In the example above we see how one organisation placed an emphasis on developing middle managers, with a focus on smarter skills, and has reaped the rewards for doing so. Continual learning has major benefits. How do middle managers place the right focus on it?

The Benefits of Continual Learning for Middle Managers and Their Teams

The benefits seem self-evident. Innovation, job satisfaction, career growth, organisational resilience, and many more. Why is this particularly relevant in the modern world of work?

We examined the concept of learnership in Chapter 6, highlighting the need for middle managers to continue to learn and adapt. It is relevant here because it is a transformative approach that redefines leadership as an ongoing, dynamic process of learning, and evolving through that learning (Monk, 2025). Middle management, like all other management positions, contains no final Boss Level or End Game, following which you have completed it. There is no completion, only continual learning, and growth. Only through continual learning can middle management stay relevant and resilient. A strong learnership culture directly contributes to employee engagement, talent retention, motivation, and productivity, as well as a sense of purpose and belonging (Monk, 2025). It is also linked to adaptability and resilience as we have already discussed in this chapter, since continual learning allows middle managers, and their direct reports and teams, to develop such things.

But research has found that this is not a widespread concept within organisations:

- 20% of managers state their organisation does not expect them to learn new things
- 31% of indicate they are not supported if they do learn new skills
- Unsupported managers are 14% less effective at coaching and identifying development opportunities, and 16% less effective at setting goals (MindTools, 2024)

Many teams rely on middle managers to identify and support their development goals and middle managers themselves rely on senior leaders for this. Organisational commitment to continual or lifelong learning is therefore paramount. In workshops I deliver to middle managers, there is always an element of holding up a mirror to the participants and asking them where they are on their management journey and how they are helping others on their journeys. We talk about how few people have all the right answers, and why it may not matter if that is the case if we have the right questions and can seek out added information, learn from it, and continuously improve. I make the point that they are a better middle manager than they were yesterday and will be a better middle manager tomorrow – but only if they reflect on their experiences, learn from them, apply that learning, and help others to grow and develop. As Monk says, "Through the practice of learnership, we will shape a new era of leadership—one that is grounded in growth, curiosity, and an unwavering commitment to learning. Let's not just lead by example; let's learn by example" (Monk, 2025).

To put this into practice, we must prioritise the learning and development of middle managers, to improve how they engage with, motivate, and grow their direct reports and teams. We should reward those who do this well. We should ensure that the content is relevant to their immediate and near-future challenges.

We need to provide learning via a range of different methods and establish a strong community of practice and identity for the middle managers to help them with coming to terms with the role and supporting work and people across the organisation. We should involve senior leaders in the programme to build better connections and relationships to organisational strategy, and we should use the programme to showcase the value and impact that middle managers can have on real-life organisational issues.

Middle managers are too important to the world of work for any of this to be left to chance. We must do better.

Case Studies

Amy Batchelor spoke to me about her time as Head of Organisational Development Projects at a large UK-based construction company. When taking on the role, Batchelor was involved in a company-wide cultural refresh. The focus initially was to improve "behavioural safety" within the culture, however this quickly grew to a full scale culture change programme including a new behaviour framework, a new way of consistently measuring business performance across all business areas, and the role of middle managers in creating a more collaborative environment and one where individuals felt respected.

In the organisation there were several development routes for middle managers in existence already. There were programmes targeted at those identified as High Potentials, and an apprenticeship programme for managers. Middle managers were part of both programmes. However, these two routes didn't consider the learning needs for most middle managers (in particular the on-site Supervisors) who needed something more succinct and not so theoretical. Batchelor was tasked with reviewing the development routes for middle managers and tying these into the wider cultural reset.

For the new development programme, Batchelor consciously avoided heavily classroom-based and theoretical/academic content. It was neither the favoured style nor approach to fit in with the cultural reset. Batchelor wanted to give middle managers confidence to manage people better, regardless of how long they had been a manager, and to do so consistently both over time and across the organisation.

Batchelor began with personality profiling and supported this with individual coaching to focus on the individuals' management journey, their values and how this aligned with their approach to management, and how to effectively manage and motivate teams whilst also managing construction projects.

From a content perspective, the programme included input on: how to manage people individually and as a team; how to motivate people; how to avoid micromanagement and getting bogged down in operational matters; how to manage through a screen (how to write emails; how to use MS Teams; how to write reports; how to use systems; how to manage time, budgets, and projects using software); and how to manage costs and stakeholders. The delivery was deliberately very experiential – focusing on real-life problem-solving, supported by some team-building activities linked to practical examples. The cohorts created their own communities of practice to support each other through and beyond the programme. There was on-demand content and micro-learning available to help provide support in real time and at the point of need.

Concurrently, Batchelor was also leading the culture change which fed into the development programme, ensuring that the new behaviour framework was weaved into the learning. A series of 3-day in person workshops were also developed as part of the culture refresh to take leaders, newly created culture champions and key influential managers through to support them in understanding the need for change, the new behaviours and how these play out within their daily roles and responsibilities. The programme focused on what great looked like in the organisation, and a tailored version was produced for middle managers. It refreshed the values and underpinning behaviours of middle managers completely at the organisation – helping to place an emphasis on how to be a middle manager rather than what middle managers do, and balancing getting stuff done with the right amount of emotional intelligence and empathy. Cultural champions were appointed and ran culture change workshops that included a lot of practical tools and templates for managers to use. A variety of additional tools, templates and activities were also produced to support the roll out to all colleagues, and the whole employee lifecycle was reviewed to ensure that the new culture was weaved in where appropriate with various processes, policies, and communications.

Upon evaluation of both the development programme and the culture change programme, Batchelor reported key behaviour changes for managers, moving from unconscious incompetence to consciously competent, with a lot of lightbulb moments shared about their past behaviour, how they had been approaching managing people and the impact it had on others. Previously, middle managers felt that to be the best in that position you had to be the loudest person in the room and be in the detail all the time. The programme changed that and showed the middle managers how to firstly look after themselves as a person and understand the values they hold close, how to hold effective, candid conversations with colleagues whilst helping them grow and develop, and how to influence across the organisation.

Batchelor is rightly proud of the impact that the programme had and has repeated many elements in her current role at a large UK luxury retail organisation. She feels that many organisations don't invest in developing middle managers and that this itself causes middle managers (and sometimes the organisation) to fail. Batchelor's programmes are about how to set middle managers up for success, and place the right focus on this tier, not just new managers or those identified as High Potentials.

Case Study Reflections

In the case study for this chapter, the following points stand out for further reflection:
–   Tying in changes to middle management behaviours to the wider culture and values can provide a useful organisational impetus
–   There are often many development routes available within larger organisations that middle management can avail themselves of, but rarely are these focused ON middle managers
–   Considering the preferred style and approach for development programmes and reflecting on whether that is relevant to the culture and values is an appropriate step
–   It can be helpful to include a wide range of content and learning methods in the development programme
–   A focus on how to manage through a screen is an understated but important part of middle management in the modern world of work, as covered in Chapter 7
    An experiential, practical focus is likely to engage middle managers more
–   Moving middle managers from unconscious to conscious incompetence (and beyond) can be awkward, but a necessary learning step in their growth

Action Plan

If you want to ensure that middle managers are prepared for the future, then the following reflective questions could help:
–   How will you create a culture where adaptability is seen as a plus?
–   How will middle managers be encouraged to formalise their reflective activities?
–   What questions will feature in check-ins that promote adaptability?
–   How will you encourage middle managers to look after their own physical and mental health? What support will be given to them for this?
–   What skills are needed for your organisation to thrive in the future, and what is the current level of these?

- How will middle managers be encouraged to consciously help their direct reports and teams to grow?
- How will middle managers be encouraged to consciously reframe situations?
- What methods of feedback will middle managers be able to access and learn from?
- What support do middle managers need to make the best use of AI?
- How will you prioritise the development of soft/smarter skills within middle managers?
- How will the expectation that middle managers continually learn and grow be set?
- What support will the organisation give to the development of middle managers?

References

CIPD (2014) *Landing transformational change*. Available at: https://www.cipd.org/globalassets/media/knowledge/knowledge-hub/reports/2014-landing-transformational-change_2014_tcm18-16180.pdf

CIPD (2023) *Are people managers doing too much, or not enough?* (2023) *CIPD*. Available at: https://www.cipd.org/uk/knowledge/podcasts/role_modern_people_manager/

Deloitte (2025) *Is there still value in the role of managers?* (2025) *Deloitte Insights*. Available at: https://www2.deloitte.com/us/en/insights/focus/human-capital-trends/2025/future-of-the-middle-manager.html

Floyd, S.W. and Wooldridge, B. (1994) 'Dinosaurs or Dynamos? recognizing middle management's strategic role', *Academy of Management Perspectives*, 8(4), pp. 47–57. doi:10.5465/ame.1994.9412071702.

Freedman, J., Miller, M. and Freedman, P. (2023) *The business case for Emotional Intelligence*. Available at: https://rw360.org/wp-content/uploads/2024/02/Business-Case-for-EI.pdf

Hudson, M. (2025) *Middle manager resilience: Lessons from coaching on leading through uncertainty*, *Forbes*. Available at: https://www.forbes.com/sites/michaelhudson/2025/04/30/middle-manager-resilience-lessons-from-coaching-on-leading-through-uncertainty/

Kapoor, A., Lenga-Kroma, J. and Kyle, K. (2025) *Learning for a skills-based future*, *Deloitte United Kingdom*. Available at: https://www.deloitte.com/uk/en/services/consulting/blogs/2025/learning-for-a-skills-based-future.html

MindTools (2024) *Building Better Managers*. Available at: https://www.mindtools.com/thought-leadership/reports/building-better-managers/

Monk, E. (2025) *Learnership: The Quiet Revolution in Leadership*. Available at: https://www.linkedin.com/pulse/learnership-quiet-revolution-leadership-edmund-monk-flpi–xy4me/

Olsen, A. (2022) *To fix workplace culture, Fix Middle Management. here's how*, *World Economic Forum*. Available at: https://www.weforum.org/stories/2022/08/boss-workplace-culture-support-middle-management/

World Economic Forum (2025) *Future of jobs report 2025*. Available at: https://reports.weforum.org/docs/WEF_Future_of_Jobs_Report_2025.pdf

Index

Academy of Management Executive 6
Action Learning Sets 32
adaptability 115–117
Allton, Diane 55, 88
Alvesson, Mats 40
artificial intelligence (AI) 24, 42, 72, 83, 101, 103, 113, 118, 121–122
Ashcroft, Rob 106–107

balancing act
– Carlin, Jo (European HR Director) 3–4
– Cheyne, Ryan 4–5
– collective duties and responsibilities 4
– community of practice 5
– culture and values 2
– focus on people 8–9
– goal-related conflicts 8
– layers 2
– middle management role 6
– pressure on teams 7–8
– professional/technical knowledge 2–3
– sense of isolation 5
– strategic directives into team-specific goals 7
Batchelor, Amy 125
behavioural safety 125
Bottois, Anwen 21
Bradley, Rick 31–33
Bridges' Transition Model 45, 60
business-as-usual challenges 37, 44

change management and communication skills 14, 44–45
Chartered Management Institute (CMI) 31, 47
Cheyne, Ryan 4–5, 11
coaching
– developing individuals and teams 87–90
– essential skill for middle managers 83–84
– learnership 90–91
– middle management responsibilities 85–87
– skills and perspectives 94–95
– tools and techniques 91–92
community of practice 5, 13, 17, 23, 27, 34, 41, 55, 66, 75, 80–81, 86, 95, 111, 112, 125

Contact Centre Manager at Yes Insurance (Ledden) 41
continuous learning
– benefits 123–125
– culture 90, 118–120
Cookson, Gary 100
Core Skills for New Managers 32
Covid-19 pandemic 8, 88, 89, 97, 107, 110
critical leadership skills
– artificial intelligence 42
– change management and communication skills 44–45
– emotional intelligence (EI) 43–44
– resilience 45–46
– skilled middle managers vs. business outcomes 42–43
culture change 126

decision-making 29–30
Dickerson, Craig 75
difficult conversation frameworks 14

essential skills in middle
– data usage 29–30
– Head of Learning and Development (Bradley) 31–33
– identify and build 34
– overcoming misalignment 31
– translating strategy into action 20–22
Emmott, Adrian 49–51
emotional intelligence (EI) 43–44
– benefits 81
– and communication 77–79
– empathy and effective communication 72
– employees job satisfaction 69
– human elements 72
– painful and public divorce 69
– and resolve conflicts 75–77
– self-awareness 68, 73–75
– technical skills and knowledge 72
– transformational leadership style 70–71
emotional proximity 24
emotional regulation 115

https://doi.org/10.1515/9783111713526-009

Employee Experience Manager at Knight Frank (Yawor) 92–94

face-to-face environment 96
financial appraisal techniques 14
Fines-Allin, Craig 12
Floyd, Steven W. 10

generative AI 11, 13, 30, 91
Gjerde, Susan 40
goal-related conflicts 7, 8
Gorman, Meg 68–69, 98–99

Halton Housing (HH) 110–112
Hancock, Bryan 11–12
Harvard Business Review (HBR, 2021) 2, 21, 36, 44
Harvard Business School 39
Head of Learning and Development (Bradley) 31–33
Head of Organisational Development Projects (Batchelor) 125
Head of Talent Development at Optimo Care (Wood) 28–29
high-performance culture 46–47
Hirsch, Wendy 60
Holmes, Nick 78, 123
HR Business Partner (Patchett) 37–38
HR Director at Informa Festivals (Parks) 79–81
Hubbard, Wendy 69–70
Hughes, Sue 110–112
human-centred approach 71, 73, 99, 104
human contact 24
hybrid working
– asynchronous/synchronous 100
– collaboration 96, 101–102
– communication 100
– critical leadership behaviours 108–109
– effective 113
– inclusion 102–103
– productivity and accountability 105–107
– and remote 96–100
– team-bonding and relationship-building 100
– technology and data 103–105

injection education 32

knowledge management systems 14, 27, 85, 102
Kotter's 8-step model 63, 65

Leadership and Performance Coach at Yorkshire Water (Emmott) 49–51
leadership building
– balancing managing up and down 40–42
– case studies 65–66
– co-ordinating and aligning tasks 37
– critical role, middle managers 37
– emotional intelligence and resilience 36
– helping, middle managers 51–52
– high-performance culture 46–47
– HR Business Partner (Patchett) 37–38
– influence without authority 39–40
– Leadership and Performance Coach at Yorkshire Water (Emmott) 49–51
– morale and engagement 62
– senior teams 36
– stakeholders in goal setting 36
– strategies to align teams 60–61
– tools and frameworks 63–64
– top-down 36
– trust in middle managers 47–49
Leadership Development consultant (Bottois) 21
Learning and Culture at Avalere Health (Holmes) 78
Ledden, Wayne 41
Lewin's Unfreeze-Change-Refreeze Model 60

Making Hybrid Working Work (Cookson) 100
management agreement 105
Managing Directors Advisory Council 12
McKinsey 7S tool 14
mentoring
– developing individuals and teams 87–90
– essential skill for middle managers 84–85
– learnership 90–91
– middle management responsibilities 85–87
– skills and perspectives 94–95
– tools and techniques 91–92
micro learning methods 74–75, 126
Microsoft Viva 14
middle management challenges
– balancing act 2–6
– decision-making 2
– future 127–128

– lack of empowerment 2
– unclear authority and influences 2
– undervalue 9–10
middle management role
– capability building 11–12
– case studies 14–17
– change champions 54
– change manager 53
– change sponsor 53–54
– helpful tools, frameworks and systems 13–14
– HR/OD/L&D professionals 54
– people managers 54
– positional complexity 17–18
– professionalization 13
– reducing the administrative burden 10–11
– senior leadership *vs.* front-line employees 53
middle managers, managing impact
– boundary management 22–23
– bridging communication gaps 25
– check-ins 24
– developing and supporting 27
– leveraging technology 24–25
– managing down 26
– managing up 25–26
– network connections 23–24
– reality 1
MindTools research 27
Monk, Ed 90
motivational theories 14

operational management group 15
operational managers 15
organisational change, role of middle
    management *See* middle management role
organisational ecosystem 55
organisational goals 6, 20, 26, 30, 31, 46, 53, 122

Parks, Nancy 79–81
Patchett, Hannah 37–38
Power Bases model 39

resilience 45–46, 120
resistance
– communication 58–59
– empathy 58
– involvement 59–60
return to office (RTO) 6
role distancing 40, 51

self-awareness 26, 43, 51, 68, 73–77, 80, 81, 115,
    120
senior teams *vs.* middle managers 20
sense-making 56
Situation; Behaviour; Impact (SBI) 92
social learning 107
softer/smarter skills 5, 108, 122–123
stakeholders
– collaborate and communicate 83
– middle managers 36
– organisational 22
storyboards and story walls 61
360 feedback tools 14

Total Shareholder Return (TSR) 4
Training Industry 24
Trust Equation 106

UK-based charitable organisation (Allton) 55, 88
UK public sector organisation 119
UK's Institute of Leadership and
    Management 15
UK's National Health Service (NHS) 69–70

Women's Employee Resource Group 117
Wood, Rachel 28–29
Wooldridge, Bill 10
World Economic Forum 118

Yawor, Megan 92–94
Yorkshire Water's People Leader
    Pathway 49–50

www.ingramcontent.com/pod-product-compliance
Lightning Source LLC
Chambersburg PA
CBHW070355200326
41518CB00012B/2241